Schools
for the
21st Century

For John Shambra, school principal, Los Angeles.
You exemplify the dedication, perseverance, courage
and commitment of thousands of teachers who give
their best to help young people find meaning
in a complex and demanding world.

Schools
for the
21st Century

EDUCATING FOR THE
INFORMATION AGE

Jeremy N. White

Lennard Publishing

First published in 1997 by
Lennard Publishing
a division of
Lennard Associates Ltd
Mackerye End, Harpenden
Herts AL5 5DR

e-mail: jwhite@nettec.net
web site: www.schools21stcentury.org.uk

A catalogue entry is available from the British Library.

ISBN 1 85291 136 0

Jacket design: Paul Cooper Design
Editor: Kirsty Ennever
Production Editor: Chris Hawkes

Printed and bound in Great Britain by
Butler & Tanner, Frome and London

Contents

Foreword

This book highlights the widespread failure of the education system to prepare young people for employment. Restrictive practices, low expectations, outdated attitudes and the demands of higher education result in thousands of young people leaving school each year with no qualifications. Disheartened, disillusioned and ill-equipped to participate in a knowledge-based economy, these young people face a future of limited options and often become a burden on society.

I have focused on three main themes: the failure of the educational system to teach students the skills they need to make it in the career world; how society can make the educational system work; and finally how technology can play a role in helping restructure today's schools.

There are numerous examples of dramatic improvements in educational performance when parents, teachers, employers and politicians are prepared to challenge the traditional orthodoxy and embrace new ideas. Failure of so many young people is not inevitable. By applying new teaching methodologies, redefining the curriculum to develop employability skills and embracing the highest standards of school management, I believe we can dramatically improve the education system.

PART ONE

How our education system is failing us. What education provides and what is needed.

Chapter 1

Education: is it meeting the needs of society?

'We are now learning a lot more about learning and we know that a lot of people with very high intelligence levels learn better in practical settings. We also know that practical skills now require a higher order of thinking. So the old dividing line between vocational and academic is fast becoming blurred and will become more and more meaningless as time goes on.'
President Clinton

Facing the 21st Century

In the year 2031 my son will be my age. He might even see the turn of the 22nd century, as may many of his friends. With the advances of medicine we can be sure that millions of babies born now will live through the next century. The 21st century is likely to see more dramatic and faster changes than ever before – new technologies, powerful emerging economies, political upheaval and radical shifts in the balance of economic and military power.

Our education system is failing to provide an adequate foundation for huge numbers of young people and appears unable – and even unwilling – to address the needs of a rapidly changing world. The proof is manifest in the millions of unemployed, alienated from society and angry that they have been cheated out of learning the skills needed for participation in the economic process. As the guardians of tomorrow we must find ways to improve our education system so that we are giving young people the best possible chance of a rewarding future.

In the process of reform we should start by asking some difficult and searching questions. What do we want our society to be like when our children are our age? How will our children make a living? How will they enjoy themselves? How will government operate? Such questions could take us into a wide debate about the structure of society in the future. The issues are complex, however it seems probable that most people will want to earn an adequate living, live in safety, enjoy a degree of economic and political freedom and thus to have a sense of participation and fulfilment. Clearly an education system that fails to provide a basic set of employment skills breeds discontent, dissatisfaction and frustration amongst school leavers if they are unable to find work. The unemployable underclass of the next century may well become a dangerous and destabilising force unless we reform the structure and process of schooling.

The present system is failing to deliver a quality service to hundreds of thousands of pupils. The brightest and richest pupils are often well served, particularly by the private sector, but the majority of pupils leave school with unimpressive results and a significant minority leave with nothing to show for years of effort.

If people are denied the chance of participation in the economic process, they are denied a series of rights that affect every aspect of how they live. Without work most of us couldn't support a family. We would suffer low self-esteem and be severely restricted in our choices of where we live, how we spend our leisure time and even what we eat. To be gainfully employed in this age of the 'knowledge worker', people need a level of qualifications, skills, appropriate habits and attitudes that are world-class. The education process plays a vital role in the development of these work related attributes and consequently directly affects people's employability. For most people education and employment are directly linked and this book is concerned with the millions of school leavers over the next decade who will be denied any chance of ever finding gainful work and participating in the economic process unless schools change. The problems are solvable but only if there is the political will to make hard choices. We must restructure the process of education so that excellence in vocational learning has the same status as traditional academic achievement.

There is certainly no room for complacency. Hungry new competitors are eager to take our share of world markets and the emerging nations are training and educating at a frantic pace. India is emerging as a world-class software producer and China's electronics industry has labour costs of about one-fiftieth of ours. We must reform our education system to ensure we provide the skills to participate in a more competitive world because we can only compete on expertise never on price.

The International Labour Organisation has warned that within 30 years Germany will have more pensioners than workers. In Britain, there are two workers for every retiree at present and the balance is changing rapidly as our 'retired' population grows. Similar trends exist in most western industrialised nations. How will we support an ageing population in the first quarter of the 21st century? How will the one in nine young people leaving school this year without formal qualifications, ever find work? How are they going to support this expanding group of pensioners, if so many young people can't find work, who is going to support them?

These are difficult questions. After searching for the right answers over the last 20 years I have come to the conclusion that our education system, based on an outdated and ineffective 19th century model, is failing us now and has no chance of meeting our needs in the new millennium. This book discusses what action we must take, to improve our chances of success as we face ever more aggressive international competition and increasingly high expectations of society from the younger generation. Dramatic reform of the education process is the only practical course. The alternatives are dangerous. Anti-free-traders, such as the late Sir James Goldsmith, who advocate protectionism through trade barriers to stem the tide of low cost imports, are more likely to harm our international competitiveness by forcing prices and unemployment to rise. Will the restriction of more efficient work practices, advocated by some trade union leaders, improve our level of employment? I fear not – Luddism never stops progress.

My son is six years old. In the year 2050 he may be sitting in an office, if anyone works from an office, surrounded by technology that we can only imagine from science fiction films. Will he look back and say that our education system prepared him for the first 50 years of the 21st century? Will his job be recognisable to someone who worked in the 1990s? In 2050 he will be 60. Today most 60-year-olds have already retired, and the age we stop work is continuing to drop. Today's retiree, according to actuarial figures, will live 20 to 30 years after he or she finishes formal employment, and our life expectancy continues to rise. Will today's education system have prepared my son's generation for half their life out of work? How will he view his primary and secondary education? Will we have made the right decisions for him? Will he smile or be sad if he concludes that his parents' generation was unwilling to abandon discredited learning methods that were useful for training Victorian civil servants, but hardly relevant to a 'knowledge worker' in the 21st century? We must take action now to prepare our children for a dynamic future so that they have the best chance of participating in the economic process.

A London *Times* headline in January 1996, *Uproar over test failures by 11-year-olds*, described how school test results showed that more than half of all 11-year-olds were not up to standard in English and mathematics. Of the 600,000 pupils who took part in the tests in summer 1995, 56 per cent failed to reach the standard in maths, 52 per cent were below standard in English. Science did better with 70 per cent reaching target. In Britain

40,000 16-year-olds (eight per cent of the school year group), leave school every year without even the lowest academic qualification – a grade G at GCSE. In 1994, nearly 80,000 pupils in English and 90,000 in mathematics did not achieve grade G – the level expected of an average 11-year-old. Are these young people well-prepared for the 21st century? What work will they be capable of performing in 2050?

Such debate is not a modern phenomenon. Antoine Nicolas de Condorcet wrote *The Progress of the Human Mind* in 1793, a treatise on humanity. Consequently he was condemned as an enemy of the French Republic, arrested and later died in jail. An aristocratic intellectual and reformer, Condorcet was an outspoken adversary of the Church and hereditary nobility. His grand vision for the future has in part come about; for example he forecast achievements in medicine, epidemiology, genetics, geriatrics, social insurance, women's rights and education. Sadly, Condorcet's comments on education are still applicable today. He observed that most societies tended to decline because of a great difference between the rights allowed by law and the rights that the citizens actually enjoyed. Condorcet identified three main factors that caused the decline of a society: inequality of wealth, inequality of status and inequality of education. You may agree that both Britain and America exhibit significant inequality in all three of these areas.

What is wrong with the current system?

I start from the premise that almost everyone wants and needs to participate in the economic process. To do so they need a set of skills and attitudes. Yet our education system is failing to develop those necessary skills because of its burdens of academic snobbery, politicisation in our schools, too many disinterested and disillusioned teachers, and an inappropriate and outdated product. Denying people the chance to gain employment is to handicap them – ensuring they are likely to become a burden to the rest of society. We have no right to go on failing future generations as we have failed so many in the past. Today we are paying the price for our short-sightedness with the huge cost of state unemployment benefits and other welfare payments, as well as the rising cost of crime. We need to rethink the purpose of education and design curricula that equip people with the skills they are likely to need to participate actively in the economic process. Young people must leave school ready, willing and able to be employed, with a foundation for the essential process of life-long learning in the rapidly changing world of the 21st century. Without a highly educated and productive work force, the UK will find it very difficult to maintain its position as a significant world economy.

The application and use of technology is already important in most jobs and will become essential in the next decade. Alarmingly, a wide gap exists between the haves and the have-nots in their level of new technology skills. Those who use computers are overwhelmingly in full-time work, have undertaken higher education and come from ABC1 social groups. In contrast those who have not are often in part-time work and from C2, D and E groups. Leaving school with limited computing skills is, and will continue to be, a severe handicap.

Too many teachers are failing to educate adequately hundreds of thousands of young people. A significant percentage of the 'profession' is highly unionised, self-interested and performs at an unacceptably low level. Market demands are ignored, ever-increasing funding and status are expected. If many teachers live by the rule that performance and productivity are irrelevant, how can we expect our students to believe any differently? Students see teachers continuing to receive pay rises by turning to the government, their unions protect poor performance and tenure ensures that the laziest and most incompetent cannot be removed. Educators continue to fail to accept that significant performance improvements are possible and that additional funding is not the answer. Today more than ten percent of children leave school without a qualification, after at least 12 years of formal schooling. It is time to take dramatic action.

The traditional role of schools in teaching academic skills and knowledge has left little time in the curriculum for the development of a realistic understanding of the modern world of work. Today's student has a limited grasp of the functions of various kinds of economic institutions, let alone the career opportunities within them and their expectations of employees.

Success and failure

Education is a fascinating subject. It is full of contrasts, of success and failure, of vision and myopia, of self-sacrifice and self-interest, of dedication and abdication of responsibility, of hope and disillusionment. Our success at training some of the world's most able scientists, engineers and bankers is well documented and so is the tragedy of tens of thousands of illiterates leaving school each year. Some leave school with glittering prizes (Britain produces more Nobel prize-winners than any country after America), others end their schooling without ever passing any public examination.

Ironically, success later in life is often preceded by early indications of little potential, with those branded as failures achieving the highest office – John Major is a case in point. Thousands of young people leave school with a deep sense of community while others have no compassion or sense of duty at all. Some school leavers are disillusioned at 16 yet become energised and ambitious by the age of 30. For others the complete reverse is true. At the Prince's Youth Business Trust, for example, which helps young unemployed people to start their own businesses, many of the budding entrepreneurs have been given a raw deal by their schools, yet still retain the determination to succeed. However, we are seeing failure on a massive scale: a doctrinaire education establishment is turning out vast numbers of young people unable to cope with the demands of a sophisticated industrialised society.

Politicians talk endlessly of improving matters and every political leader promises reform. It is hard to think of a recent politician who hasn't pledged to put education at the top of the agenda – yet we see hardly any progress, and the little there is seems to benefit the able and better off. As the Chief Inspector of Schools has said, 'We know how to solve the problems but do we have the political will?'

The tragedy is that this failure is unnecessary. Educationalists and politicians, mostly from the professional middle-classes, have resisted change because their children are doing adequately, often in expensive fee paying schools. But to ignore the need for change is to fuel an angry group of malcontents with a steady steam of recruits. Those whom the system fails have few choices. Most of those choices are dangerous and costly for the rest of society. Some school leavers who have the barest qualifications will go on to get work, take training and be brought back into the fold. But others, hundreds of thousands of others, will drift towards state dependency or, worse, turn to criminal activity to meet their financial expectations.

The 1996 HM Schools Inspector's report about Britain's worst schools reported that 'inspectors found problems with poor teaching compounded by bad behaviour, high truancy rates and large numbers of expulsions, even among infant children. We accept that these problems stem from poor teaching and school management, we do not accept that "modern teaching methods", whatever this general term is supposed to mean, are the problem.'

There is ample evidence of the state of affairs. According to HM Inspectors, reading standards in primary schools need considerable improvement in one in 10 schools and writing is substandard in one in seven. The Inspectors found that by age 11 too many pupils still remained reliant on their fingers for counting, were unable to use a ruler correctly and were wildly inaccurate when making assumptions. According to a study of the National Curriculum examination results by the Social Market Foundation, the average gap between the best and worst primary schools in the same authority was found to be four years in English and over five years in maths. The report also highlighted that almost half of all 11-year-olds are below the basic standards in maths and English. In 1997 only 15 out of 14,500 primary schools had all their pupils up to the government's designated standards.

According to Chris Woodhead (*The Times,* 6 March 1996) one of the most disturbing problems we face is the poor performance of white working-class boys. They are the least likely to participate in full-time education after the age of 16 and are the most likely to leave compulsory education without qualifications. Girls seem to be doing better than boys in almost all subjects. In tests given to 7-, 11- and 14-year-olds, girls are doing better than boys and are more successful in every subject including traditionally male areas such as design and technology, computing and chemistry. For the under performing white male group in schools serving the most disadvantaged areas, less than 15 per cent of pupils are achieving five or more GCSE A to C grades.

It must not be forgotten that despite the loudly heralded improvements, the majority of young people leave education by the age of 18. While 72 per cent of 16-year-olds are in full-time education, only 58 per cent of 17-year-olds are, and only 30 per cent of young people go on to higher education. (DfEE Statistical Bulletin 7/95; DfEE Press Notice 26/96)

Truancy is an indicator of underlying problems, just as absenteeism at work often tells a story about management and company motivation. At any one time in Britain, 80,000 pupils are absent from school, according to the union Unison, whose members represent the education welfare service. Unison's officers, who are charged with catching offenders, claim that about 10 per cent of the school population play truant at some time during the academic year. (*Financial Times,* 18 October1995)

Educational problems usually start at primary level. A child who has not learned to read in primary school is much more likely to play truant later on and have on-going school problems. Growing awareness of the failure of many primary schools has been highlighted by Ofsted's recent findings that one in five of the seven-year-olds in three London boroughs achieved no score at all when tested.

It is not all doom and gloom. The 1997 annual report of the HM School

Inspectors names 30 outstandingly successful secondary schools as models of what can be achieved. Astonishingly 25 per cent of the schools are grammar schools even though they account for less than one per cent of all schools in England and Wales. Sadly much of the left-wing debate is about how to get rid of these examples of excellence in education. The British Labour Party, with its huge parliamentary majority, must encourage thousands more schools to aspire to the high standards of teaching achieved in the 163 grammar schools and the private schools, rather than criticise these schools for being successful. In the corporate world our best businesses are not closed down on the basis that this will help our worst ones. We look to the best to teach us how to improve the rest.

There are calls in both America and Britain to privatise the education system. Indeed the benefits of privatisation have been demonstrated in numerous other areas. Why should education be different? It is time to eliminate tenure; to hold teachers accountable for their students' test scores and emulate the most successful teaching methods.

The changes we need

This book is not about cataloguing the shortcomings of the current system. It is about finding ways in which an outstanding educational system can be achieved – one that gives everyone a genuine chance to succeed. The present sham of egalitarianism could hardly be more divisive.

The impetus for the changes we need is unlikely to come from the government or the Department for Education and Employment, or from teaching unions or academic educationalists. It is more likely that change will result from the efforts of innovative education reformers – activists in schools and businesses across the country who see the failure of the current system and who realise that tinkering with an outdated model is pointless. Just as the steam car of 1900 was replaced with the new technology of petrol engines, rather than by better-designed steam cars, no amount of re-engineering will make our outdated educational structure suitable for the 21st century. Pupils need to be taught by a new generation of enlightened teachers, by whom they are encouraged to have innovative ideas, to use their imagination, think and act independently, and to learn in an environment where they can challenge the system and test new ideas,

We love learning and being informed: millions of us watch the news, listen to the radio and browse through a newspaper. Learning is fun – yet millions loathe their experience of school. Too many young people are turned off learning because their school experience is dull and irrelevant.

Schools are dictatorial and authoritarian, offering a sharp contrast to our national democratic structure and the way most families interact. The result of this contradiction, not surprisingly, is widespread alienation. We need a school environment where young people develop their interpersonal skills such as team work and leadership and the ability to think creatively and laterally. The development of personal characteristics such as enthusiasm, commitment, perseverance and flexibility must be encouraged. Students must leave school enthusiastic about continuing their education throughout their lives.

What should society expect?

Society expects a great deal from the education system. Fully employable school leavers, internationally competitive workers, low levels of juvenile delinquency – the list goes on and is unrealistic. Clearly educators are not directly responsible for causing or having to solve all of society's ills. We should expect educators to focus on providing the best service possible with a shared responsibility for the outcome of their efforts. What we expect our schools and colleges to provide is complex, but I believe we can agree on several key elements.

(i) A fundamental requirement is that school leavers or college graduates should have a basic set of skills that will allow them to secure and retain a job. It is difficult to participate in the social and economic life of a developed nation unless you can earn a living. For most of us, our sense of self-worth and belonging revolves round our work and our ability to sustain ourselves and our families. When we describe ourselves, we more often than not start with a description of our work.

(ii) School leavers should have an understanding of how our social and economic systems work and their own role and responsibilities in society.

(iii) They should have a set of values that reflect the present national sense of right and wrong and an optimism about life's opportunities.

(iv) Because ongoing training and personal development is so important, our school leaver needs the motivation to return again and again to the learning process.

By identifying the foundation skills and information-processing requirements that those most at risk need, we can then adjust the curriculum to fill the identified gaps. In other words, teach skills that will enhance the chances of becoming employed. The Edwardian economist, J.A. Hobson, saw education as a route to opportunity. He said, 'What is needed is not an educational ladder, narrowing as it rises, to be climbed with difficulty by a chosen energetic few … it should be a broad easy stair that is wanted … one which will entice everyone to rise.' So often, those who are against reform speak of declining standards. Critics bemoan youth crime and unemployment, yet restrict the way out of social impoverishment supporting an elitist educational structure with a narrow specialist curriculum. They are against vocational education, describing it as second-class, and reject the idea of a broader, more practical education such as that provided in countries like France, Germany, America and Japan.

International comparisons

The failures of our education system are by no means an exclusively British phenomenon. A fresh look at education is an urgent priority in all industrialised countries. The US has significant problems and may be an indicator of the difficulties we can expect in the UK. For example the New York school system, the largest in the USA with 1,095 schools and over one million pupils, has major problems. In 1995 New York schools had a budget shortfall of £150 million despite taking a quarter of the city's total budget. Teaching standards are reported to be poor and school crime is soaring: during the 1994–95 school year 19,814 crimes were reported – 16 per cent higher than the previous year (*The Economist*, 7 October 1995). The Californian education system, the second largest in America, ties with Utah as having the most crowded classrooms, with an average of 27 pupils per class according to the State and 34 according to the Teachers' Association. California ties with Louisiana for the worst academic results in the nation.

Research by Skillsbank USA in June 1996 found that nearly half of the United States' 191 million adult citizens are not proficient enough in English to write a letter about an invoicing error or capable enough in mathematics to calculate the length of a bus trip. In 1992, according to a report to Congress, approximately 3.4 million individuals in the United States between the ages of 16 and 24 had not completed high school and were not currently enrolled in school, representing approximately 11 per cent of all individuals in this age group. The report also added that threequarters of high school students in the United States enter the workforce without a degree, while many do not possess the academic and entry-level occupational skills necessary to succeed in the changing United States workplace. Surprisingly, most dropouts are not from the stereotypical background of the inner city. Seventy per cent are white and 30 per cent are from the inner cities. According to the US Department of Education (NCES

1993) 87 per cent are from English speaking homes and 68 per cent have two parent families.

The primary educational system of the United States is in serious need of reform. In a 1996 survey, less than 50 per cent of US adults understood that the Earth orbits the sun yearly, while only about nine per cent knew what a molecule was. (Survey of National Science Foundation, *Columbus Dispatch* 24 May 1996). America has the least efficient educational system in the industrial world, spending $5,500 per pupil, and producing the lowest quality output as measured by reading skills. Surprisingly for the world's leading capitalist country, the American education system is the epitome of socialist experiment. It is essentially 100 per cent government-controlled, its workers are unionised, their leadership demonstrates disdain for the free market system, and their output is deplorable. In the recent NEA (National Education Association) handbook, readers are told to 'alert Association leaders and members to the dangerous convergence of organisations with political, religious, or economic agendas now striving to ... substitute market competition and market driven values for public service.' The highly politicised NEA has backed numerous non-educational issues including pension funds, clean water, reproductive freedom, feminist and gender equity issues, and gay, lesbian, and bisexual issues, while opposing Trident II missiles, Judge Robert Bork, home schooling, aid to Nicaraguan rebels, and the religious right. In addition, they issue a publication titled *Extremism Watch*. The majority of their legislative agenda does not even address children, with only $1 out of $6.24 going to children, the rest going to social security.

It seems that the 'American dream' does not mean an education system that encourages the development of enterprise skills, rather to many American educators it is the quest for a higher minimum wage, higher welfare benefits, stronger unions, and greater government control. It appears to me that American teachers, like their British counterparts, teach subjects with little relevance to the 'real world', and often fail to teach children about capitalism and the free market principles that made the United States the world's strongest economy.

American educators that fail, are as difficult to sack as their British counterparts. 'In New York it costs an average of $194,520 for each dismissal case and lasts on average 476 days. In some cases, the legal bill has reached $900,000.' (*Columbus Dispatch*, May 1996)

International comparisons are difficult but research indicates that some countries such as Japan, Singapore and Switzerland are doing much better at educating young people. Teaching methods appear to be the main reason, where more time is spent on foundation skills rather than higher level thinking skills. The Third International Maths and Science Study (TIMSS report) looked at educational achievement in 41 countries. English school children ranked 25th in maths and 10th in science, significantly behind Singapore, Japan and Korea. Rich East Asian countries did extremely well in maths taking the top four places. Money seems to have little impact on achievement. American children, who have three times as much money spent on their schooling as South Koreans, did significantly worse.

Are standards falling?

We often hear the cry 'standards are falling' and read headlines such as 'New Universities Offer Places to Students Who Failed A-levels'. Are these charges valid? Certainly there are far more people going on to higher education. In the early 1960s, only the top five per cent of pupils went to university: now, over 30 per cent attend higher education. Commentator Dr James Tooley of the Institute of Economic Affairs has even suggested that less people should pursue higher education: but just because more people have the opportunity to do so, this does not mean that the top five per cent are doing worse or that standards have fallen. Historically many able young people were denied the chance of a university place because of their social background or poor schooling. Apart from a broader range of subjects being on offer, many more pupils are passing A-levels and delaying the search for work by continuing their education. Examiners maintain that the tests are as difficult as ever and there is little evidence to show otherwise.

According to a report by three learned bodies – the London Mathematical Society, the Institute for Mathematics and the Royal Statistical Society – our students are, however, becoming less numerate. Their report, *Tackling the Mathematics Problem*, found serious deficiencies. In a test taken by a group of undergraduates specialising in maths, 95 per cent were unable to calculate the area of a portion of a circle. In another test taken by a group of the most able 14- to 16-year-olds, only 20 per cent knew how to work out a simple percentage. As calculators are widely used in schools this means that the students didn't even know how to solve the problem by pressing the appropriate buttons. The former Secretary of State for Education, Gillian Shephard, made an attempt in 1997 to bring more rigour to maths examinations by proposing a ban on the use of calculators. But blaming the use of calculators rather than sub-standard maths teaching is not an effective way to improve maths standards.

Where does the failure to teach even basic material leave the slow learners? The Engineering Employers' Federation has expressed this concern, saying that the lack of basic literacy and numeracy makes training enormously expensive. The general consensus of a survey of 1,000 managers by the Federation was that they had to spend too much time rectifying the deficiencies of the schooling system. But where should the blame fall? According to the Mathematical Society's report, much of it lies with new teaching methods introduced in the early 1980s. The report calls for a return to old-fashioned teaching methods, where five-year-olds chant their multiplication tables, while older children memorise mathematical proofs.

A *Sunday Times* article entitled *Britain's Worst Schools* (16 April 1995) stated that bad schools have common characteristics – ineffective head teachers who lack clear policies, combined with poor parent-teacher relationships. The article added that schools are plagued with poorly qualified teachers who lack communication skills and have low expectations of their pupils' performance. Home work, if done, is inconsistent and irregularly marked. Rules are arbitrary and inconsistent and money is wasted on pet projects. Clearly, the structure is wrong in these terrible schools. Often run by a cabal of governors and staff, they suffer from weak management and a lack of leadership.

In the country's worst schools, up to a third of the pupils regularly miss lessons. Absenteeism of teachers is also an issue. A 1995 study found teachers were more likely to take time off than pupils. The *Sunday Telegraph* reported some areas where a typical teacher missed 14 working days out of 190 because of sickness, while pupils were only absent four days a year.

Chris Woodhead, Britain's Chief Inspector of Schools, found in his 1995 annual report that about 25 per cent of school children are being let down by their teachers' low expectations, lack of knowledge and progressive teaching methods. The problems were most acute in primary schools, with almost 30 per cent of lessons for children aged 7 to 11 and just under a quarter in the 5 to 7 age range being judged by inspectors to be sub-standard. In the worst school, about 50 per cent of the teachers were judged unsatisfactory. The report, based on visits to 1,000 schools, estimated that there were 15,000 bad teachers who should be sacked. In our union-controlled, tenured system, it appears that there is very little that can be done to remove the teachers who are harming our children's future. If there is truth in the adage that one rotten apple spoils the barrel, what about a barrel where a third of the apples are rotting?

Woodhead's report criticises poor teachers for spurning traditional methods in favour of modern approaches. But I disagree. A modern approach isn't the problem: bad teaching is the problem. We often mistake 'modern teaching' for a lack of discipline. But the enemy of good teaching is poor subject knowledge, low expectations of pupils, poorly run lessons with little structure and an inability to manage and motivate a classroom of pupils.

Increasing levels of participation

Participation in post-16 education and training has increased in the UK, but the rate of increase has been slowing down. The 1996 School Leavers' Destination Survey shows the proportion of 16-year-olds remaining in the education system fell slightly from 83 per cent to 81 per cent in April 1996. The proportion of 16-year-olds going into full-time education in England fell at the same time from 68.1 per cent to 67.6 per cent – though the numbers continued to rise because of the increased size of the teenage population.

A large number of young people do leave full-time education at 18; about 30 per cent proceed to higher education. It seems likely that those who have done badly at school will be reluctant to continue with life-long learning, thus reducing their prospects even more.

The House of Commons Education Committee has recognised that young people are making critically important decisions earlier. The committee focused their recent review not on 16- to 19-year-olds, the traditional grouping base of the examination structure in Britain, but on 14- to 19-year-olds – acknowledging that work-based training may be appropriate from an earlier age.

Participation in higher education is also improving. As already noted, nearly a third of all young people now go on to higher education, and student numbers have almost doubled since 1988–89. The type of student is also changing with more mature students and students studying part-time attending university today. Forty per cent of entrants to higher education come through routes other than the traditional A-level programme.

Life-long learning

A society that encourages life-long learning will be more competitive. There is a growing political and industrial consensus in Britain that if international competitiveness and social cohesion are to be achieved, there has to be a transformation of attitudes towards attaining skills and then learning new ones.

Professor Charles Handy introduced the idea of 'new training agents' analogous with good theatrical or literary agents. They could advise their 'clients' on opportunities to expand their skills, thereby rendering them more marketable. Employer-led training may not be enough to meet the needs of those who are outside long-term, full-time employment.

Student support should also encourage life-long learning. Sir Geoffrey Holland, the Vice Chancellor of Exeter University and a former Permanent Secretary at the Department of Employment said, 'If we had a system of individual training or "learning accounts" or whatever they are called in later life, the learner or potential learner can call on those when she or he chooses, either part or full time.' An even more radical idea is a tax-exempt, portable, personal training fund that could be topped up by employers, the state or the individual.

The role of technology

Young Britons, in comparison to their European counterparts, appear more IT literate. The percentage of homes in Britain with computers is higher than in North America – 50 per cent of homes with teenagers have a computer, and most school leavers are proficient in the use of computer technology. Schools, however, are still significantly under-equipped in comparison to businesses. According to the Department for Education and Employment, two out of every five school computers are more than five years old and access to the Internet and its vast range of on-line services is limited. Prior to the 1997 election, David Blunkett, now the Secretary of State for Education, pledged another £150 million for technology in schools.

There is a widespread misconception that the application of technology in teaching is a luxury that comes after the learning of basic literacy, yet in fact the reverse is true. Technology should be used to improve basic literacy; it is part of the solution. Computers can be powerful learning tools. A third of young people cannot spell the word 'sincerely' and more than 40 per cent spell 'apologise' wrongly, according to Nick Tate, the UK government's chief curriculum adviser. Yet spelling can be taught efficiently and inexpensively using computers, while word processors can highlight mis-spelling and poor grammar to improve writing skills.

Perhaps society expects too much from our education system. Some will cry that parents, community leaders and politicians all have responsibility for creating the society we need, and that therefore the burden cannot be put on teachers and schools. Of course the causes of our problems are multi-dimensional and the solutions complex. This book is about how schools can better serve society.

Adapting to changes in the labour market

We face two shortages: a shortage of jobs and a shortage of skilled labour. To maintain our share of world trade, we must explore ways both to reduce unemployment and to increase the number of skilled employees.

Schools can do a much better job at preparing people for work, equipping them with skills that will improve their employability, and enhancing their chance of finding the best possible job. For too long teachers have denied this essential role of education; in my view, education for education's sake is a luxury to be enjoyed *after* students have acquired the basic skills for employment. Young people must be better equipped for work. The education process must ensure that young people have the necessary level of skills that will allow us to retain our position in an increasingly globalised market, and most important, allow people to participate in a meaningful way in our society.

Labour markets are changing. The way in which we work, the application of technology displacing the low-skilled, the need for larger numbers of highly trained technically skilled workers, the end of a lifetime in one career or a job for life – all these factors have significant implications for education and training. Forward-thinking commentators recognise the need for successful economies to be built on a learning society, in which initial education prepares people not only for societal participation and work, but also for the need for continual training and re-training. The government endorsed the importance of ongoing learning by setting National Targets for Education and Training which were introduced in 1991 and revised in 1994.

The Confederation of British Industry in their survey *Tackling Long-term Unemployment* said '... (our) survey of employers confirms that the labour market is undergoing major changes. As the pressures of competition and improvements in technology intensify, sectoral shifts in employment will continue.' The report's key findings identify a lack of skills, a problem of which the long-term unemployed are aware but are unwilling or unable to address. 'For while the majority of long-term unemployed people believe that they are hard workers, quick learners and willing to work flexible hours, almost half reported that they have not been equipped by the education and training system with literacy and numeracy skills. Thirty-two per cent believe that they do not have any useful qualifications.' The report goes on to say that it is clear that unemployed people do not know enough about how the job market is changing and how they must respond.

Despite high levels of unemployment, however, most trade associations and industry bodies report that their members find it difficult to fill vacancies. A report at the AGR conference in 1995 found that 40 per cent of employers had some difficulties in recruiting. Many commented on the poor quality of graduates, while those who identified specific skill shortages pointed to interpersonal skills, such as communication and teamwork, as being in short supply, followed by commercial acumen and leadership.

The British Labour Party recognises the need for change and issued a consultation document in 1996 setting out proposals for young people. Labour's twin objectives are to 'substantially reduce youth unemployment, and improve the skills levels of those aged 16 to 25 years old'. The paper went on to say, 'Without action we will continue to pay a heavy price in welfare bills and lack of skills, damaging the prospects of the economy as a whole and of business in particular.' (Business Consultation Document, Education and Employment Opportunities for Young People. Labour Party 1996)

Work in the future – enterprise skills

If, as seems to be the case, there is a general consensus that pupils should learn about business, why don't schools teach skills such as entrepreneurship, business management and marketing? Why do educational institutions refuse to talk about the vital role of business in society, about the job prospects that their pupils may face and about how pupils can enhance their skills to enable them to participate in the economy? Part of the answer is that teachers know little about the demands of the workplace, and even less about the skills needed to start your own business. Even worse, political dogma blinds many to the real needs of their charges.

The House of Commons Education Committee stated in their 1996 report that: 'The importance of improving the UK's effectiveness by creating a more skilled workforce has long been recognised, and many of the issues, such as the need to enhance the vocational and occupational skills of young people, or the need to increase participation of young people in post-compulsory education and training have been discussed many times.' The committee recognised the need for change and highlighted some of the dramatic societal changes that have taken place since World War II. In the past it was assumed that only a small percentage of school leavers would stay on for further education. Now about 70 per cent of 16-year-olds stay on for full-time education compared with less than 48 per cent only 10 years ago.

The significance of youth unemployment

If it is true that the education system is failing to provide large groups of people with the skills they need to participate in the economy, what exactly is the scale of youth unemployment? In 1995, of the nearly two million registered unemployed in the UK, half were under 30 years old, and some 400,000 had been out of work for six months. In 1994 there were over one million people aged 18 to 29 claiming unemployment benefit and one million young people aged between 16 and 25 were out of work (British Youth Council Figures). Youth unemployment is significantly higher for ethnic minorities. In London the unemployment rate for black males aged 16 to 24 is a shocking 62 per cent and young black men are three times more likely to be jobless than young white men. Even for those who have graduated the difference for ethnic groups is stark. Unemployment for ethnic minorities stands at 14 per cent compared to five per cent for whites (Terence Braithwaite, Coventry University). Although unemployment has come down significantly in the last two years the problem of finding work for low skilled young people remains significant. Such problems are not a uniquely British issue but are taxing politicians across Europe and in the United States.

For those excluded from economic participation, the attraction of criminal behaviour will grow as a means to make an income. The human need to belong will be met by membership of gangs, which offer the benefits of belonging to a social group even if the gang behaviour is anti-social and criminal. This is not a depressing forecast for the future, but is the reality in cities such as Los Angeles, Atlanta, Miami and New York, and increasingly in certain parts of the UK. There are numerous studies of youth delinquency which give a good understanding of the scale and nature of the problem. From these studies we can see that the reduction in opportunities for young people with limited educational backgrounds to take part in learning constructive responsibility through employment, is a significant cause of anti-social behaviour.

There is some good news. Between 1980 and 1992 the number of students in higher education doubled from 340,000 to 690,000. The proportion of school leavers without graded GCSEs or their equivalent more than halved between 1975 and 1991 (DfEE). However, it is the problems of the under-achievers which must be highlighted and ways found to help those who are most at risk. The middle classes, who do quite well in school, have a good chance of finding employment and enjoying some of the benefits of economic prosperity – but even they could have a much more useful education.

We are failing, as the large number of long-term unemployed young people illustrates, to develop the full potential of hundreds of thousands of students, the majority of whom are poor, disadvantaged and from the ethnic minorities. In Britain, according to research by the Prince's Youth Business Trust, unemployment for people age between 18 and 29 increased from 1.8 million in 1991 to 3.1 million in 1993. This increase of 64 per cent was composed of a significant number of the low-skilled and untrained. Unemployment has fallen in the last two years (1996–97), in part by redefining the classification of long-term unemployed, but the experience in other European countries would suggest this is not sustainable. France, for example, has 10.9 per cent unemployment and Germany 12.5 per cent. Average earnings in the UK are just £18,300 a year.

Most employers will confirm that whilst youth unemployment is high, they have difficulty filling vacancies because the skill levels of many applicants is so low. The head of personnel at Los Angeles-based Pacific Telesis, a Fortune 500 company, tells the following story. His company interviewed 3,000 applicants for entry level vacancies – as trainees, both technical and administrative. Only 300 applicants could pass the basic entry test for literacy and numeracy. All 300 were hired. After three months, 30 remained with the company. With 100,000 young people leaving school in Britain each year without a GCSE in maths or English, the same story could be told by many UK employers.

Demand for change

A growing tide of interested parties are demanding change from the education service – better teaching, more relevant curricula, improved skills training, attention to the demands of both pupils and society, and better value for money. If we fail to meet these demands the UK economy will decline, losing market share to stronger and more dynamic competitors. The consequent social costs of failure to reform will be rising crime, civil unrest, drug dependence and even higher levels of unemployment.

Chapter 2

Education: is it meeting the needs of employers?

'Education is hanging around until you've caught on.'
Robert Frost (1874–1963)

Changing pattern of work

Work patterns are changing. The concept of a job for life is outmoded, and employment is characterised by uncertainty and change. Periods of work will be mixed with time spent in retraining or unemployment. Today's graduates need new skills to find a job: they need to be flexible so that they can constantly acquire new expertise and maintain their employability. Modern employment demands expertise in such areas as team work, computer knowledge, problem solving and information research and processing. Low skill, high cost jobs are moving to low cost production areas such as Mexico, China, Taiwan and India. Frustrated by skills shortages, militancy, government regulation and other anti-employment restrictions, companies are constantly searching for alternatives to employing people – thus the highly regulated economies of Europe and America are most vulnerable. Recently, for example, Daimler Benz announced that it would no longer manufacture vehicles in Germany, preferring less regulated countries for assembly activities. Not only are aggressive emerging economies taking Western jobs, so is technology, and these new threats are unlikely to retreat. The UK's large clearing banks average one staff member per 100 customers: in comparison the new 'direct' telephone banks have a ratio of one staff member per 1,000 customers. We are powerless to stop these changes. Our education system must adapt to meet the needs of employers' future jobs, not the jobs of yesterday.

We need to understand where the new jobs are likely to come from and what skills they will require. Only then can we develop curricula that address our learners' needs. In 1991 the Small Business Administration in America reported that big business had shed two million jobs and at the same time small firms had hired 4.5 million new employees. All the net new jobs have come from small firms. The trend is the same in Britain. Clearly, a strong start-up and small firms sector remains our best hope for the next generation, though large firms will of course continue to develop. In the service sector, new jobs will be relatively low-skilled, but employers will expect minimum levels of interpersonal skills and self-management. Whatever the trend in minimum wages, these low skill jobs will not pay well. To win the highly competitive, high-skill, high-pay jobs, today's school leaver needs a complex set of abilities that are provided by few educational establishments.

Self-employment may well be the only option for millions of workers, yet we have no formal requirement for the curriculum to teach enterprise or business skills. Most school leavers can't tell you what an invoice is, let alone a profit and loss account or a balance sheet, or anything about basic marketing, sales, production or the simplest principles of employee management. In fact all the foundation skills of management are missing from most pupils' education.

Few educationalists seem to recognise the urgency of the need for change. If we do nothing, the ranks of the unemployed will grow, especially amongst those who are unskilled. After a year of unemployment, entering the work place becomes much more difficult. The only option for many people will be sporadic, part-time work, some participation in the black economy to top up their income, and ultimately welfare dependency.

Ways of working have changed dramatically in the last 20 years. Britain must compete in the global market place. Computers are on most managers' desks, bar code scanners, fax machines, mobile telephones and satellite communication impinge on the working lives of millions of employees. Although only 25 years old, computer chips are everywhere. Today there is hardly a car on the road built after 1988 without at least one computer. In 1996 Mercedes Benz models had on average 10 microchips – their latest vehicles have over 50.

Companies now expect their employees to exhibit greater willingness to adapt to new conditions. Vice-President Al Gore, personally associated with the 'information superhighway' recently said, 'By the year 2000, 60 per cent of the new jobs in America will require advanced technological skills,' adding that, '… while our work places are moving swiftly into the information age, our classrooms are not keeping pace.' Self-employment is thus emerging as the only option for hundreds of thousands of people who are, in today's terms, 'unemployable'.

According to the UK's Department for Education and Employment, 1.5 million people already tele-commute and the numbers are increasing at seven per cent a year. A recent National Opinion Poll (NOP) estimated that 30 per cent of companies now have employees working from home or who plan to do so. Research conducted by the American Institute for the Study of Distributed Work shows that three to five per cent of the US work force telecommute already and the figure is expected to hit 10 to 15 per cent by the year 2000. The study also indicates that a teleworker enjoys a 16 per cent increase in productivity regardless of the nature of the job (*Director Magazine*, October 1995). Clearly these levels of improvement in productivity will encourage the development of new ways of teleworking. Already new video conference technologies are influencing how we work and the remarkable growth rate of the Internet will open up many new opportunities.

A massive project designed and implemented by one of the world's biggest companies, General Motors, illustrates how technology is being used in today's workplace as well as showing the level of information that school leavers are going to have to use at work. General Motor's Computer Aided Maintenance System (CAMS) is what is called an expert system, designed to know how to maintain and repair your GM car. A central computer at GM headquarters is linked to dealers' service bays throughout the USA, and it is always ready to help the mechanic repair the car. It can take information straight from the vehicle's own on-board computer, diagnose the problem and offer detailed instructions for repair. The time taken to repair a car has dropped by two-thirds and the chances of getting it right first time have improved dramatically. CAMS has a form of artificial intelligence so that it is constantly learning – by comparing fault information it can improve its diagnostic reliability and look for patterns of faults. The computer and the mechanic are both in a learning loop, and remarkably, so is the car, because its computer chip can be regularly updated with new diagnostic software. GM have found that the CAMS system is a highly effective teaching tool for developing the skills of their thousands of mechanics. (*Schools Out*, Perelman L.J.)

It is remarkable that a comparable learning process cannot be found in any school. The feedback loops just don't exist. Certainly there is testing, but no attempt is made to rectify the shortcomings which become evident. Imagine GM repairing faulty cars but doing nothing with the information about what is wrong. Finding a production problem, would they blame the home environment of the factory employees or demand that the government give them more money?

In their book *Competing for the Future*, management commentators Gary Hamel and C.K. Prahalad describe the sort of management thinking that we need to develop in order to compete successfully in the future. They suggest that an innovative, problem-solving approach needs to be nurtured and developed by schools so that graduates are not 'programmed' to cram facts for a test, but to bring fresh ideas to existing problems (Harvard Business School Press: September 1994):

'If the goal is getting to the future first, rather than merely preserving market share in existing businesses, a company must be much more than customer led. Customers are notoriously lacking in foresight. Ten to 15 years ago, how many of us were using cellular telephones, fax machines, and copiers at home, 24-hour discount brokerage accounts, multi-valve automobile engines, compact disc players, cars with on-board navigation systems, hand held global positioning systems, automated teller machines, MTV, or the home shopping network? As Akio Morita, Sony's visionary leader puts it: "Our plan is to lead the public with new products rather than ask them what kind of products they want. The public does not know what is possible, but we do. So instead of doing a whole lot of market research, we refine our thinking on a product and its use and try to create a market for it by educating and communicating with the public."'

As these examples illustrate, business is applying technology at many levels within the organisation. In contrast, schools lag far behind in IT implementation.

There isn't a school in Europe with one computer for each pupil, yet an estimated 80 per cent of all salaried workers will work at video display terminals by the year 2000. (Pat Billingsey, *Hard Test for Soft Products*, SIGCHI Bulletin, Vol. 27, no. 1, January 1995.)

Foundation skills for work

A 1996 report by Ofsted, the schools inspection agency in Britain, reported that the reading level of four out of five seven-year-olds was below the average for their age. In the report of 166 lessons observed, the inspectors found that nearly half had 'unsatisfactory or poor teaching'. As we have seen, literacy and numeracy are basic skills that all school leavers need, both to find and hold a job, yet hundreds of thousands of young people leave school without them.

By evaluating the skills involved in work we can develop a more useful educational curriculum. A study in the United States (SCANS) identified three 'foundation skills' and several 'competencies' that students are most likely to need either in their further education or when going directly into work.

According to SCANS, there seems to be little evidence that schools are producing students who are better equipped for the transition from school to employment despite numerous commissions and reports. For example, of the thousands of young people who apply for grants to the Prince's Youth Business Trust (a charity that has helped over 30,000 unemployed young people start their own businesses), very few have the basic training in running the simplest business and face a steep learning curve in their first endeavour. The result of this is a failure rate of over one third in the first few years. Two thirds of the start-ups do survive, a high rate by national standards, but the waste of energy and resources of those who don't make it is enormous. Improved vocational education, that included basic business skills development, would almost certainly improve the chances for these start-up firms.

We need to be aware of the vocational education debate in the United States. The US is one of our major competitors for world market share. President Clinton, in his GOALS 2000 bill submitted to Congress in April 1993, stated that there is a need to 'establish a National Skill Standards Board to promote the development and adoption of occupational standards to ensure that American workers are among the best trained in the world'. Richard Riley, the US Secretary of Education, stressed a similar theme: 'We need high standards. In an international marketplace and an information century, countries meeting world-class standards will have the edge. By encouraging educational reform across America, we will help create a high-skill, high-wage workforce that is the best in the world.'

The SCANS 'foundation skills' are reading, writing and arithmetic, required for almost every job. In America, there are 90 million Americans lacking these basic skills and in Britain an estimated five million people are functionally illiterate. It is obvious that problems at this level will severely restrict the employment opportunities of many school leavers. The ability to exhibit higher level skills of thinking and reasoning, and inter-personal qualities, differentiate between those likely to find employment and those who will not. Sadly these higher level skills receive little development or attention in our schools.

The 'competencies' identified in the US SCANS report include skills that make an employee more valuable to the organisation, for example, the ability to work in teams, evaluate data and use technology.

Research by Winter and Hawlkins examined the skills needed by graduates in the 21st century. One of their initial findings was that the 'biggest requirement for successful individuals, now, and in the future, is for them to have the skills to manage uncertainty.' (AGR Conference, UMIST, Manchester 1995). The message is that good jobs will increasingly demand people who can put knowledge to work. Yet the evidence in the 1991 SCANS report, and numerous press articles, suggests that more than half of all high school graduates are without the knowledge or foundation skills to find and hold a job.

The skills that employers want

Although most teachers are not anti-business, many are out of touch with the needs of employers. As the two cases below illustrate, major employers focus on a very different set of skills from those developed in our schools.

Grand Met Trust (renamed Tomorrow's People), part of Grand Metropolitan, the food and drinks giant that owns Burger King, Häagen Dasz, Pearl Vision and hundreds of international brands, recently published a document entitled *What employers want from the school or college leaver*, to help stimulate dialogue and practical action between schools and colleges and their local businesses. Grand Met believes in the importance of closer links between local schools and employers. Educationalists tend to focus on the knowledge and skills that are perceived to be appropriate to the world of work. Employers, on the other hand, will often try and identify an appropriate blend of knowledge, skills and personal qualities or character traits.

Grand Met identifies nine 'skills' that are important in the workplace:
1. **Knowledge concepts and skills.**
2. **Communication skills:** at the basic level, the ability to make yourself understood and to act upon other people's communications – listening, speaking, giving instructions effectively and clearly are all important.
3. **Literacy skills.** The pattern of literacy skills mirrors that of communication. All school or college leavers should be comfortable with accepted English grammar and should be able to spell and punctuate competently. At the higher levels they should be able to follow a detailed written argument and to use written language as an effective tool – particularly to inform and persuade.
4. **Numeracy and accuracy.** In essence this means being comfortable with figures. Grand Met emphasize that this does not mean the application of abstruse mathematical formulae: indeed for the majority of jobs, the four functions plus the ability to calculate percentages will suffice. Numeracy

involves the ability to spot anomalies and to draw valid conclusions from the figures. Accuracy is essential. Errors can go unchallenged for a long time and confidence drains away once errors are identified.

5. **Computer literacy.** This will soon become an essential requirement for many if not most jobs: the ability to input data into a system or to extract information from it, together with a broad awareness of the capabilities and limitations of electronic processing. Closely linked to this are keyboard skills that are equally necessary in their own right. The revolution that has taken place in office, clerical and administrative work has put an increasing emphasis on keyboard familiarity, which can generally be easily learned.

6. **Time management skills.** Detailed supervision in business and manufacturing industry is becoming less relevant and therefore less practised. Staff are required to manage their own time to work to deadline, to complete tasks or to fulfil the responsibilities assigned. This in turn makes the ability to plan time and to prioritise effectively of greater importance. To some extent this is covered by examination planning in school. However, there is little evidence that even basic time management skills are taught as a formal course in any school or college despite the sophistication of modern practices in this area and the enormous advantages of using the techniques.

7. **General knowledge.** Employers want school or college leavers to have a basic general knowledge of how society and business work and of those political, social and economic systems and processes that have an impact on the citizen. They also want the youngster to understand the importance and role of profit and wealth.

8. **Specific knowledge.** Employers are concerned to encourage the ability to acquire knowledge – they are sometimes less interested in the knowledge that has already been acquired, since it can be irrelevant to the particular work situation.

9. **Physical care and fitness.** Looking after yourself, taking pride in your physical well-being will help raise morale and reduce stress. Work by Professor Jonathan Fielding at UCLA in the USA found significant reductions in absenteeism when anti-smoking and healthy eating campaigns were organised in companies and illustrates the importance of employees having an awareness of health issues.

After knowledge skills, Grand Met have identified eight personal qualities and attitudes that are important to an employer:

1. **Energy and motivation.** Any school or college leaver who convinces the

employer that he or she is genuinely motivated to succeed and who will be energetic in pursuit of success is virtually assured of a job providing that the employer is confident that his energy can be harnessed. This is an important statement from one of the world's major employers, and is an obvious contrast to the teacher at a comprehensive in South Yorkshire who told me that he saw little point in his pupils learning about business because they wouldn't be able to find work anyway. Grand Met go on to add that they wish to see competition as part of the experience of all young people in education because it is a fact of life in society and especially in business. So much for the attitude of some left-wing councils in Britain who ban competitive sports because competition is in some way unnatural and unfair.

2. **A willingness to learn.** Most young people profess a willingness to learn, but the employer needs this to be a consistent commitment for a period of years. Given this commitment, employers will then be more likely to commit themselves to regular training and updating. I often saw people in my own companies who refused to take training courses; they had left school with no qualifications and as a consequence had lost all confidence in their academic ability. These successful managers were too ashamed to participate in a training course with their peers for fear, always unfounded, of appearing foolish.

3. **Integrity.** This is more than straightforward honesty, the necessity for which may be taken as read. It is caring about what you are asked to do in your job – having concern for and pride in the quality of the outcome of your work.

4, **The inquiring mind.** The desire to question the *status quo*, and to challenge constructively. The inherent belief that there is a better way and that it is up to the individual to identify it. What a contrast to the autocratic nature of school where to question is to risk being branded as a trouble maker. Hardly the right environment to encourage constructive challenges as a way to better decision making.

5. **Reliability.** An inherent self respect which motivates the youngster to honour his or her undertakings.

6. **Social skills.** These will enable the school or college leaver to play an appropriate part in a team and to interact with others effectively in different settings and under pressure.

7. **Respect for others.** Involves the ability to see things through the eyes of other people and will encourage businesses and teams within businesses to make equal opportunities a reality.

8. **A sense of humour.** This will make life easier for everybody.

Grand Met and other leading employers want a complex set of skills from their employees. When we contrast those needs with the ability of the lower performing school leaver it is hardly surprising that so many young people find it impossible to find satisfying work or even a job at all.

Let us look at another large employer, famous for its quality control, high standards of service, staff development and customer focus. Marks & Spencer is a worldwide retail chain with more than 600 stores and 62,000 employees. Of these, 52,000 are based in the UK.

Kate Orebi Gann of Marks & Spencer's personnel department in London describes how the education process affects many new employees. For the largest group of employees, the sales staff, there are no academic requirements for entry. Marks & Spencer will not discriminate against anyone if after 12 or more years at school that person has come away with no paper qualifications.

For a management entry job, the company looks for some qualifications in maths and English and A-level standard grades as a minimum. To land a trainee management job at Marks & Spencer is no mean feat. In 1996, there were 8,500 applicants for 275 places. Applicants had better have something to offer over and above a few paper qualifications. Kate explained that what the company looks for are personal qualities. She said she has seen some improvement in the project work that schools are undertaking, but the decline of cross-curricular activities and the lack of awareness in schools of the work place were cited as a problem. There should be more teacher placements and increased employer involvement in education, as well as higher quality career guidance, in Marks & Spencer's view.

Sales staff application forms list the characteristics that Marks & Spencer consider important:

1. **Job motivation:** To what extent are activities and responsibilities in the job likely to provide the applicant with personal satisfaction? The questions probe for extracurricular activities at school or college and any holiday jobs or other work experience.

2. **Teamwork:** Does the applicant show a willingness to participate as a full member of a team and to contribute even when a task may be of no direct personal interest? The interviewer is encouraged to probe the applicant's involvement in group activities, teams and voluntary work. The company looks for evidence of participation, enjoyment working with others and an ability to develop harmonious relationships with colleagues.

3. **Adaptability:** The ability to respond positively and effectively to changes and unexpected developments. What changes has the applicant

experienced and have they reacted positively to them? Do they accept change as a necessary part of life and are they likely to adhere to company systems and procedures?

4. **Stress tolerance:** What is a prospective employee's stability of performance under pressure and would they have the ability to make controlled responses in stressful situations? The interview examines ability to relax, acceptance of criticism, amount of energy, ability to overcome problems and cope with stress.

5. **Work standards:** Ability to establish and maintain high standards of performance. Has the applicant set high personal standards and do they take pride in what they do? At this point an applicant's academic achievements are discussed. One interesting and rather telling question is 'How do you think your exam results reflect your true abilities?' – a wide open question for those who may have struggled with the deadening examination process.

6. **Confidence and oral communication:** Does the would-be employee act in a confident manner and can they express themselves clearly and effectively? It is interesting to note that this is about oral not written expression, the skill least trained and tested in school. Even higher education provides little or no training in communication skills and public speaking – a task every manager has to perform at some time. Politeness is a characteristic that the interview assesses – a vital skill in any business or organisation. How many school pupils are trained in communicating in an 'open and friendly style' and communicating with confidence and self-assurance?

The above criteria are used for all levels of applicants to Marks & Spencer: a definite contrast to what is emphasised in the school classroom.

The management application form is supported by a series of selection criteria. How many of these are truly taught and developed in the modern school? The questionnaire includes planning and organisation, assertiveness, leadership, job motivation and analytical skills. The analytical skills don't focus on solving equations or working out trigonometry, but rather on real world practical skills – analysing situations, identifying issues, gathering relevant information and drawing logical conclusions. Awareness and teamwork, recognising the impact of one's own decisions, taking account of the feelings and needs of others in order to build relationships and form effective teams – all these factors are important. Employers frequently seek the ability to work as a member of a team: in British schools teamwork is often called cheating and can be severely punished.

The Marks & Spencer management application form is seven pages long. One page is devoted to academic qualifications while the other six look at personal characteristics and work experience. Thus their priorities are clearly indicated, and they represent a significantly different set of learning objectives from those developed in schools.

Parents, pupils and employers alike must be confused by the bewildering array of qualifications – an estimated 14,000 in Britain compared to less than a thousand in France. Such a plethora of qualifications makes value comparisons extremely difficult, particularly of those considered 'academic' versus those that are 'vocational'. Their respective purposes are not always fully understood. For example, in its submission to the House of Commons Education Committee, a spokesman for J. Sainsbury plc said, 'It is a bit like Sainsbury's offering 14,000 lines for sale (the typical number in a medium sized supermarket) without providing customers with any information about where to find the product they are looking for to meet their needs, and second about its fitness for purpose.' He added, 'In general, many employers are bewildered and confused by the range of qualifications held by prospective employees.'

Flexibility and adaptability will characterise work in the 21st century. We will have to learn to cope with a rapidly changing work environment, multiple careers and periods of self employment and unemployment. These are the realities facing today's school children.

The importance of the small firms sector

Although much political debate and news concerns large firms, the small firms sector is a vital part of our economy. When we talk about preparation for employment we often think of jobs in big organisations. The truth of the matter is that today's school leaver has about a one in five chance of going to work for a small firm or being self-employed. In fact the ratio continues to decrease. In the next 10 years, 25 per cent of the working population may well be self-employed or working in the small firms sector. We should be teaching the basic skills of running a business to vast numbers of students so that they can improve their chances of finding work, and make a greater contribution to the business when they do so.

Interestingly, any growth in employment comes from the small business sector, with millions moving into self-employment. There are many definitions of a small firm. The Department of Trade and Industry uses in its annual report the definition from the Bolton Report of 1991, 'a small firm is an independent business, managed in a personalised way by its owners or part owners, and with a small market share.' Typically, small firms have less than 10 employees.

Few people realise the significance of the small business sector to the British economy. For example, 97 per cent of all businesses employ less than 20 people, and 91 per cent presently employ less than 10. More than two-thirds of the companies in this country consist of one or two people. Seventy-eight per cent have a turnover of less than £100,000 per year and a remarkable 98 per cent have sales of less than £1 million. Just think of that – all those famous businesses that you know, account for only two per cent of all of the businesses in the UK. Of the 15 million companies in Europe, only 12,500 employ more than 150 people – that's less than one-tenth of one per cent.

In 1991 there were four million self-employed people and one million small, limited companies. Small firms employ more than a third (36 per cent) of the private sector work force, and they produce nearly a quarter of the gross domestic product. In the European Community, there are 15.7 million small and medium size enterprises and 16 million self-employed. (Federation of Small Businesses)

Between 1983-93, small business created 2.5 million new jobs. During the same period large firms were shedding jobs. Between 1993 and 1994 the top thousand firms laid off one million people and 90 per cent of all new jobs came from small firms.

In Britain, from 1985 to 1989, firms employing fewer than 20 people created over a million additional jobs – that was at least twice the number as large firms. The change over the last 25 years has been significant. In 1979, small firms accounted for 27 per cent of the workforce but by 1991 that figure had risen to 33 per cent. The number in self-employment during the same period rose even more dramatically from 1.9 million people to 3 million – up by 70 per cent. The increase was even greater for women – female self-employment doubled between 1981 and 1993.

So where does all this information about small firms and self employment lead us? When educators think about how they can help their students prepare for work, they need to be aware that those without qualifications are obviously not destined for a leading law or accountancy firm. Nor are they necessarily going to work in the local McDonalds. We know that up to a quarter will join the ranks of the self-employed whilst a few may even aspire to the success of businessmen like Yorkshireman Sir Graham Kirkham, who left school at 16 but recently took his company public with a value of £300 million. Tim Roots, who sold his computer firm for £7 million, left school at 16; his school reports said that he did not work hard enough and he failed all eight O-levels.

Chapter 3

Education: is it meeting the needs of individuals?

'Education is not preparation for life: education is life itself.'
John Dewey (1859–1952) American philosopher and educator

Failing the individual

Research carried out by the Office for National Statistics in 1997 found that almost half the adults in Britain lacked the necessary reading skills to use a bus timetable or follow the instructions to assemble a bicycle. Clearly education is failing to provide millions of people with the everyday skills they need.

Having considered the expectations that society and employers have of the education system, let us now examine what individuals require from it. Young people who have recently left school have been called 'Generation X'. (I can offer no explanation of this name or who coined it, but it is a term in common use. It is generally taken to mean the generation born between 1961 and 1978.) In this chapter we consider the views, fears and aspirations of 'Generation X' (see *Generation X: Tales of an Accelerated Culture*, Douglas Coupland 1992). From a better understanding of the 'consumer', perhaps we can develop educational products that meet young people's needs rather than the needs of their parents or even grandparents.

In a fast-moving, complex world people need constantly to acquire new skills. They need to develop a sense of community and personal responsibility, to learn how to learn, and to acquire skills that make them employable. Perhaps most important of all, they must develop the ability to work with others. These are the things that young people need and want to learn.

It is clear that we are failing to give many young people a useful education. Pupils' needs are largely ignored and their frustration and dissatisfaction is self-evident. We need to stop trifling at the margins and take significant action to transform an inefficient and ineffectual education system. This, of course, is easier said than done.

But what can we do for the 40,000 young people who leave school every year without qualifications, or for the 80,000 whose basic English is inadequate? One suggestion from Sir Ron Dearing, the government's Chief Curriculum Adviser, is to develop easy entry routes to further education colleges, where those who have dropped out of school might respond to a more adult environment.

When a student has failed his exams, schools continue to move such pupils to the next year until the time comes for them to leave. Examinations, part of the 'quality control system' check pupil progress, much to the annoyance of the teaching unions, however there is no mechanism to rectify any shortcomings. Thus learning problems and teaching problems are ignored rather than solved – the antithesis of the model of modern business organisations.

Many young people feel that the educational system is failing them. Whilst unions and politicians dally over minor details, the greatest worry for Generation X is the fear of unemployment. Most of us would agree that a school leaver with few or no qualifications, who is functionally illiterate and innumerate, has limited prospects of participating in the employment market. The individual is being sold short.

Sir Claus Moser, an Oxford don, raised the issue of declining educational standards in a well-publicised speech at the Royal Society of Arts. Moser said that Britain's education system was lagging behind Western Europe and the Far East. He identified four main concerns:
1. Illiteracy – a serious and disgraceful problem. In national tests of 11-year-olds, only 44 per cent reached the expected level in English.
2. Innumeracy – schools paid too little attention to arithmetic and British nine-year-olds were rated third from bottom in a table of 14 countries.
3. School buildings – many children were left in 'appalling conditions'. A survey estimated that £3 billion was needed over the next five years just to keep schools open.
4. Vocational education courses – these left the workforce short of 'middle-management qualifications', crucial to economic success.

The group in Britain least likely to participate in full-time education after the age of 16 are white, working-class boys. They are the most likely to be completely without qualifications when leaving school. On a brighter note, girls are doing much better in national curriculum assessment at all ages. Even in the traditionally male subjects girls do consistently better, with the exception of physics. In a report by the Chief Inspector of Schools about performance in the most disadvantaged areas of the country, less than

15 per cent of pupils achieved five or more GCSEs grades A-C. Even the best schools in these areas achieve scores which are about one third of that to be found in schools in more prosperous areas.

There are many theories about why pupils are doing so badly in these often poor inner city areas – the lack of education of parents, the number of single parent families, the difficulty of attracting good teachers to poor areas, disruptive pupils, disillusioned staff – although the cause is probably a combination of these factors. There is no doubt that the education system's performance is an abysmal failure for these unfortunate children.

Attitudes of Generation X

Most of the people making decisions about the education of teenagers are over 40 and many are in their fifties and sixties. The world of teenagers is of course significantly different from 20, 30 or 40 years ago, as it is with every succeeding generation. However, a 'we know what's best for you' approach cuts no ice with the 1990s teenager.

Today's young people are the children of the 'baby boomers', those who were children in the 1960s. The attitudes of parents play a major role in shaping the attitudes of their children. This generation has a low, but an increasing level of higher education with 40 per cent of 16- to 18-year-olds staying on in full-time education. And the students are gaining technical competencies, according to research by Saatchi & Saatchi – 69 per cent of British 15- to 24-year-olds can operate a computer, the highest level in Europe.

The attitude of Generation X towards family is quite different from that of previous generations. Generally they are more concerned with building a career than a marriage: the number of married 20- to 24-year-olds has fallen from 48 per cent in 1971 to 18 per cent in 1991, and also women are seeking to establish themselves in the job market before having children. The average age group for first births has risen from 20-24 in the 1980s, to 25-29 in the 1990s. This trend is expected to continue.

Culturally, music and the cinema are the main influences, with 63 per cent of 16- to 24-year-olds attending pop concerts and 81 per cent going to the cinema. Television is the universal cultural activity with 99 per cent of 16- to 29-year-olds reporting it as their top leisure activity. Perhaps reassuringly, 75 per cent of 18- to 24-year-olds had read a newspaper the day before the interview, and 37 per cent a magazine.

So how do the attitudes of young people compare with the previous generation? The attitudes of the 'baby boomers' make up the dominant values of the late twentieth century. There seems to be a feeling of 'boomer envy' amongst the younger generation, springing from the perceived difference in the levels of opportunity between the 1960s and the 1990s. The present generation has developed a strong sense of self-preservation; they appear to have lost faith in collective action, and feel threatened by the dangers of the nineties, such as AIDS, drugs, pollution and crime. Research shows that they want to carve a unique niche for themselves in the job market by finding a career that fulfils their personal desires. There is a trend towards acquiring more skills and working at a number of different jobs.

Underlying these factors is a scepticism, a cynical approach to life that can be misinterpreted as a lack of concern. Scepticism protects this generation from a feeling of vulnerability, which in turn reinforces the need for self-preservation. The younger generation prides itself on being able to see through things and people. They can be difficult to persuade and exhibit insecurity. They are wary and weigh decisions carefully, and also resent being patronised or rushed into things. Generation X's rather cynical and sceptical outlook puts pressure on those teachers who know they are not giving their best and try to hide behind their mock authority. From this cynicism, pragmatism develops, so that Generation X pride themselves on living in the real world, while having little faith in the future.

When a sample of 16- to 24-year-olds were asked what issues were most important to them, 70 per cent said having a good time and more than half said saving money. A little more than 40 per cent said their career was important, sports were cited at 20 per cent, religion less than 5 per cent and politics wasn't even mentioned. When asked about issues of social importance, unemployment was the dominant concern, with 70 per cent of respondents ranking this at the top of their list, while health and education followed at 65 per cent. At the bottom of the list family values were rated as important by only 5 per cent of the respondents.

Produced by the American Faith, the 'Popcorn Report' outlines the consumer trends of the nineties and adds to the picture by describing nine characteristic attitudes of Generation X.

1. **Cocooning:** The impulse to go inside when it gets too scary outside. Companies are responding by marketing products and services directly to the home, so that the customer does not have to go outside the cocoon. Note the vast growth in home shopping and on-line sales business.

2. **Fantasy Adventure:** The search for thrills and chills. Companies are providing virtual reality products and outdoor survival training, a dimension of this search for identity through physical challenge. Perhaps

this accounts for the increasing use of drugs such as Ecstasy.

3. **Small Indulgences:** Rewarding or pampering ourselves with small pleasures both in quality and quantity. Companies are offering gourmet products in small portions, handmade quality, and little luxuries such as aromatherapy. For example, with the guidance of the Prince's Youth Business Trust, thousands of young people have set up craft businesses and many have found good markets for well-made, small production items, often selling to their own peers.

4. **Egonomics:** The search for individuality, uniqueness and self-esteem, manifesting itself in ways that may shock an older generation. For example, the trend of body piercing and even implanting steel spikes into the scalp was featured in a *Newsweek* article (10 August 1996) and can be seen on university campuses the world over.

5. **Cashing Out:** Leaving the fast track of organisational careers to re-balance life and work on 'what is real and important'. There is a notable increase in businesses run from home. One of America's largest franchises, Mail Box Etc, serves this vast market of home business owners and they see excellent prospects for expansion in Britain and the rest of Europe.

6. **Down-aging and Staying Alive:** Refusal to be bound by the traditional age limitations and the quest for health. Consumers continually seek healthy products, plus expert information on the contents and impacts of products and services. 'A fascination with every nuance of better health.'

7. **Vigilant Consumer:** The protest generation comes of age as the generation of super consumers, finding shabby quality, corporate irresponsibility, and false marketing claims to be social injustices too close to home. Companies respond by improving warranties for products and services, publishing ethics statements, and providing 'do-good' products. This attitude has implications for schools that operate on authoritarian lines, with little or no consultation with either pupils or parents and an indisputably substandard product and service level. Even universities tolerate very limited student input when it comes to planning the educational process. It is time for educators to work out how they will respond to the 'vigilante consumers', ignoring them at their peril.

8. **Ninety-nine lives:** So many goals, so little time. This generation, the generation of mass communications, computers and the Internet, want to do so much but feel they don't have enough time. Companies are responding by selling products and services to do more in less time, to keep people on-line with information and to filter information and thus reduce the need for direct access.

9. **SOS:** Save our society, a dedication to the three critical Es – environment, education and ethics. Note the growth in recycled products and packaging and cause-related marketing (corporate support for popular charities and good causes).

The Spiegel Youth Survey of 1994 of 14- to 29-year-olds saw the youth in the 1990s as a composite of the experience of the youth of past decades: the lack of illusions of the 1950s, the scepticism of the 1960s, the radicalism of the 1970s and the hedonism of the 1980s. But the 1990s do not have the visions of any of these other decades; the report concludes that 'the youth of the nineties lives under the curse (with the blessing) of believing that all significant alternatives are futile.'

Chapter 4

The Roots of the Problem

'The direction in which education starts a man will determine his future life.'
Plato (427-347BC) *The Republic Book IV*

O
ur education system is based on 19th century principles and is
outdated. Methods of teaching are often ineffective, demoralising,
disillusioning and boring. The curriculum is of limited use for
large numbers of students, many teachers seem to fear technology, modern
management and appraisal, and as a result there is a high student failure
rate. Thousands of young people are handicapped for life, unable to
participate in the economic process because of an education system that
appears to resist moves to improve productivity and performance.

The philosopher, Professor Charles Handy, wrote in *Beyond Certainty*:
'When I went to school, I did not learn anything much which I now
remember, except for this hidden message, that every major problem in life
had already been solved. The trouble was that I did not yet know the answers.
Those answers were in the teacher's head or in her textbook but not mine. The
aim of education, in that world of certainty, was to transfer the answers from
the teacher to me, by one means or another. It was a crippling assumption.
For years afterwards, when confronted by a problem which was new to me, I
ran for an expert. It never occurred to me, in that world of certainty, that
some problems were new, or that I might come up with my own answers. I
was continually down skilling myself. I was cheating myself of my potential.'

There is a structural misalignment of our approach to schooling when
compared with that of society. Since we live in a democratic society, we teach
and value democratic principles of freedom and choice. Yet, as Roland
Meighan in *A Sociology of Educating* has pointed out, there are three teaching
styles: authoritarian, autonomous and democratic. Unfortunately the
dominant method of teaching is the 'authoritarian' style characterised by the
attitude 'You will do it our way'. One person, or at best a small group of
people, make and implement the decisions about what to learn, when to

learn, how to learn, how to assess learning, and the learning environment, often before the learners are recruited. I am sure that the inherent hypocrisy of this system does not escape the critical eye of many older pupils.

Education philosophy: academic versus vocational

Our vision of learning must be much broader than mere 'schooling'. Learning is 'the receiving-oriented learning process and involves the act or experience of acquiring and developing knowledge or skill'. As such, it is distinct from the 'sending-oriented teaching process' (imparting of knowledge or a skill), 'pedagogy' (the art or profession of teaching), and 'curriculum' (group of related courses, often in a special field of study) (*The American Heritage Dictionary, 3rd Ed.*)

One reason that schools are not meeting the needs of many students relates to curriculum issues and educational philosophy. The curriculum needs to be changed to help students become more employable and, through employment, have the benefits of attaining a degree of economic freedom. A discussion about how education can improve employability leads to the exploration of the curriculum itself, and from there to issues of the academic and the vocational. To my mind there is discrimination built into our education process because all students up to a certain age receice the same product irrespective of their needs. An academic curriculum is considered acceptable and vocational study, second class. Until we come to terms with the need for an alternative, equal status vocational product, the long overdue reform of school-based vocational training will probably not take place.

Sir Ron Dearing, the government's Chief Curriculum Adviser, has recently suggested extensive reforms of the present narrow curriculum, with its concentration on traditional subjects as a precursor to graduate studies. Sir Ron sees raising standards as an essential goal, and suggests a way to do this is through the introduction of broader subject coverage at A-level, including new vocational qualifications called Applied A-levels. This new curriculum will have similar academic standards to traditional subjects, but with less restrictions, and with a modular approach. Dearing's ideas are helping to break down the barrier between academic and vocational studies but his proposals are far from gaining universal acceptance.

There has been some progress in the UK with the introduction of General National Vocational Qualifications (GNVQs). The government has recognised that not all young people want – or are suited to – purely academic courses and have extended the provision of vocationally-based alternatives. More than 100,000 pupils at 1,000 schools are taking GNVQs and a new scheme is being piloted for children between the ages of 14 and 16.

Encouragingly Ofsted, in October 1994, found that GNVQs standards were 'broadly comparable with those at GCE A-level'.

Assessment-driven education

At present much of the school curriculum is driven by the requirements of higher education rather than those of business. As I have already pointed out, schools are trying to meet the needs of the third of their pupils who go on to higher education, at the expense of the two-thirds who go from school to work. As the majority of further education graduates will also go to work after college, I would argue that the school curriculum ignores an important need of all their students.

Our current system is driven by assessment, so that teaching is often focused on exams. While students constantly fret and worry about these tests, the learning process is being harmed. Much of the pleasure of learning is destroyed, and probably of teaching too. For students, learning should be a joy of study and exploration rather than a chore to get to the destination of an examination.

Charles Handy, in *Thinking Differently About Education,* asks:

'Why are we the only country in the world except Russia that makes every child take the same examination at age sixteen? If everybody took their driving test on their seventeenth birthday we would probably have half as many good drivers and the others not allowed to drive at all – safer roads maybe, but a lot of frustrated people. What I want to see are "standards" which, like music tests, you take when you know that you can pass.'

If we agree that people do not want to leave school angry, frustrated and feeling that their time has been wasted, why do we make sure that so many do? This is precisely what happens to tens of thousands of school leavers.

Better measures of intelligence

Part of the difficulty lies in the way we evaluate people. Let us consider two men who are, by most standards, very successful. One sold his company for millions of dollars, having a string of world-class inventions to his name, including the digital thermometer and the heart valve monitor to name two. Note that he has no degree in science. The other man, a senior manager at Microsoft and friend and colleague of Bill Gates, has made a fortune out of his Microsoft stock. He is a software engineer and has written many best-selling programmes. Similarly, he has no formal university qualifications. Perhaps more important than their financial success, these two individuals have a wide range of interests and seem happy and fulfilled in life: but judged by traditional 'academic standards', they are not 'successful'.

Academic qualifications should not be the only yardstick by which individuals are judged. A number of educationalists have described new models to help us think about intelligence and how to assess it. The traditional school focuses on testing literacy and numeracy, combined with memory testing. But there are more enlightened ways to think about intelligence. In 1983, the educationalist, Howard Gardner, concluded that most conceptions of intelligence were too narrow and should be broadened beyond the confines of the narrow book-learning emphasised in schools. He describes seven major, and relatively independent, dimensions of intelligence, thus constructing a persuasive argument that intelligence consists of multiple talents. Gardner's main argument derives from the diversity of skills found in a modern technological society. Today's world is full of people who may not score highly in verbal or logical skills but who excel in others such as spatial skills (artists and architects) and interpersonal skills (effective counsellors and empathetic teachers). Gardner's ideas make intuitive sense. For example, we all know people who don't seem terribly sharp but have excellent instincts for getting along with others. This ability serves them well, and in some instances they're more successful than their 'brighter' counterparts. Others seem very self aware and have the ability to capitalise on their strengths and minimize their weaknesses. We can presume that many pupils fail because of our unwillingness to meet their style of intelligence and learning. Pupils who do not fit into the present narrow definition of educational success are too readily branded as failures; their rich talents can be crushed in our myopic school system.

Charles Handy wrote about Gardner's philosophy:

'I want us to understand that everybody is intelligent; it is just that they are intelligent in different ways. Howard Gardner lists seven "multiple intelligences". I would list around ten: factual, linguistic, analytical, spatial, practical, musical, physical, intuitive, inter-personal, the list goes on. The point is that some of us are lucky enough to have four or five intelligences. I believe that everybody has at least one, and the job of education is to find out what it is, and to foster it, because then you will feel that you have the capabilities and have something to contribute. We send half our children out of school feeling that they are basically stupid.'

These learning differences fall into three broad categories, cognitive, affective and physiological. (see diagram opposite, taken from Gardner's *Theory of Multiple Intelligences* [Adapted from Gardner and Hatch, 1989] Educational Psychology. Eggen, Paul A.)

Dimension	Example
Linguistic intelligence: sensitivity to the meaning and order of words and the varied use of language	Poet, journalist
Logical-mathematical intelligence: the ability to handle long chains of reasoning and to recognise patterns and order in the world	Scientist, mathematician
Musical intelligence: sensitivity to pitch, melody and tone	Composer, violinist
Spatial intelligence: the ability to perceive the visual world accurately, and to recreate, transform, or modify aspects of the world based on one's perceptions	Sculptor, navigator
Bodily-kinesthetic intelligence: a fine-tuned ability to use the body and to handle objects	Dance, athlete
Interpersonal intelligence: the ability to notice and make distinctions among others	Therapist, salesman
Intrapersonal intelligence: access to one's own feelings	Self-aware individual

The qualification confusion

As previously mentioned, there are approximately 14,000 different qualifications in Britain and consequently employers are often confused about the relative value of newer courses. A basic introduction might be helpful in understanding the range and diversity of what can be studied at school.

For pupils from 14 years up, there are five main levels of qualification:
Level 1 are GCSE grades D-G, NVQ level 1 and Foundation level GNVQ.
Level 2 covers GCSE grades A-C, NVQ level 2 and Intermediate GNVQ.
Level 3 covers the traditional A- and AS-levels, NVQ level 3 and Advanced GNVQ.
Level 4 is undergraduate level, NVQ level 4.
Level 5 covers post graduate, professional qualifications and NVQ level 5.

The General Certificate of Secondary Education (GCSE), introduced in 1986, replaced the O-level. It is the standard measure of achievement for 15- to 16-year-olds. GCSEs can be taken in a wide range of subjects including, thankfully, business studies. Assessment is through a combination of course work and exams. It is interesting that this combination of more interesting and relevant material combined with modular study has led to improved examination results and sadly the complaint that the exams must have a lower standard. The GCSE is graded from A-G and a common benchmark is how many pupils at a school achieve grades A-C in five or more subjects. In 1994, more than 40 per cent reached the level of five or more A-Cs.

A-levels, established over 45 years ago, have become the 'gold standard' for traditionalists. The exam's original purpose was to select an élite for higher education. Times have changed and this purpose is questionable. As a result, too many students not suited to academic study are now taking A-level courses and dropping out.

A-levels are the traditional passport to a university education. There is much criticism of the early in-depth specialisation of the A-level and its narrow academic focus. Most students study two or three subjects and take their final exams between the ages of 17 and 18, following a two-year course. Some newer courses are modular, with term-work assessment accounting for 20 per cent of final marks. The range of syllabi is broad – 465 different ones are approved – and the grading system is A-E. About 34 per cent of British 17-year-olds are taking A-levels, up from 20 per cent in 1983. In 1994 there were 750,000 entries for the examination. The AS-level is a more recent qualification, introduced in 1986. It covers half the content of the traditional A-level. Far fewer students take the AS-level, about 50,000 in 1994.

In my view, the A-level programme needs to be much broader; Sir Ron Dearing's proposal to move to a broader curriculum is welcome, as is the trend towards modular A-levels. Many subjects are now available in either a modular or a standard format. Modular exams are assessed in three ways: via course work, end of module tests and a final examination, which must count for 30 per cent of the overall mark.

Modular teaching, however, is under fire. The editor of the London *Times* wrote on 28 March 1996: 'The other erosion of excellence is the "modular" approach to A-levels ... they allow sections of the course to be sat, and re-sat in such a way as to bump up marks overall ... arousing a strong suspicion that ... with the growth of modular teaching, the qualification is easier to acquire.' He ended the leader by adding: 'Modular teaching is the enemy of excellence and a hidden danger in an ever-more competitive world.'

A-levels are a major source of weakness in our system. Their narrowness, because of their depth, imposes premature and largely irrevocable choices at an early age. Many students drop either arts or sciences at 16, thus limiting their choice of further education and employment. The idea that a student who has specialised in two or three arts or science subjects at A-level is in any sense broadly educated is ridiculous.

A-levels were introduced when only five or 10 per cent of pupils stayed on after the school leaving age. But now, with more than 30 per cent progressing to higher education, the A-level has reached its 'sell-by moment', according to Sir Geoffrey Holland, a former permanent Secretary at the Department of Employment. The principal final-school-year qualification should not be one that is only appropriate for a minority of school leavers. The A-level examination is being stretched to cover too wide a range of pupils so that many are embarking on it even though it is inappropriate for them; frustration, failure and disillusionment is the inevitable outcome.

Yet many academics, especially those in universities, support the distinct academic route. Alan Smithers of Manchester University argues that there needs to be a 'healthy divide' between vocational and academic pathways. He argues that society needs a 'differentiated system of qualifications that caters for those of different abilities and interests'. Smithers does accept that the current three A-level specialisation is 'unduly narrowing'.

Gillian Shephard, when she was Secretary of State for Education, said in 1996, 'I think we need to retain the A-level. I think we need to retain it because it is tried and tested and in particular it is understood ... I also think the A-level is a testing examination and I think it is a very good test of academic ability, so I respect it and would not want to see it go or diminish.'

As long as A-level courses continue to be specialised, with students rarely studying more than three, we will see limited progress in the move to providing pupils with the broad foundation of skills necessary for a life time of learning and work.

A vocational form of A-level was introduced in 1992 called the General National Vocational Qualification (GNVQ). Designed to develop employment skills as well as offering a route into higher education, the GNVQ marks an important step towards a high quality vocational education for those who want to gain foundation skills for general employment. NVQs are studied in both schools and colleges and usually involve some form of work experience. GNVQ courses are available at three levels.

1. Foundation, broadly equivalent to four GCSEs at grade D or one NVQ level 1.
2. Intermediate, similar to four to five GCSEs at grades A-C or NVQ level 2.
3. Advanced, equivalent to two GCSE A-levels or NVQ level 3. Foundation and Intermediate last one year whilst Advanced takes two years to complete.

GNVQs are based on achieving competencies in particular subjects and are unit based comprising combinations of mandatory and vocational units with required core skills. The tests are assessed in several ways including multiple choice questions and projects and assignment course work that is marked within the educational establishment but with outside verification. The qualification is gaining popularity with 184,000 students registered for GNVQ courses in 1994-1995 yet the drop-out rate remains high at about a third. (Evidence to House of Commons Education Committee Report 1995-96)

In 1987 the introduction of the National Vocational Qualification (NVQ) marked an important step in the development of education in the workplace. Students study for a vast range of qualifications in 12,000 centres around Britain, many on the premises of employers.

Anti-business culture in schools

Unfortunately, our educational system shows little interest in encouraging enterprise, and provides virtually no training in the basic skills necessary to encourage the budding entrepreneur. An anti-business culture appears to persist in many parts of our educational system. Those with extreme anti-enterprise views deserve short shrift. They are out of touch with economic reality and have a narrow and regressive political agenda. We need to be aware of the danger of a small group of educationalists who consider that enterprise education has no place in the curriculum.

We read a great deal about the younger generation's negative attitude towards business and industry. A study by the Oxford University Education Department provided more details about these attitudes, finding that young people differentiate between 'business' and 'industry', where an anti-industry attitude is prevalent. Industry is seen as stereotypically dirty, noisy and polluting, and hence the cause of environmental problems. As we saw from the reports on young people's attitudes, the environment is important to them. Industry is perceived as an unpleasant and undesirable place to work: business, on the other hand, is viewed as more attractive. Self-employment is seen as more interesting than working for others. Profit is now considered a positive and important element in business, although there are misgivings about 'excessive' profit. Perhaps through the many programmes that link businesses to schools there will be an improved understanding of the complexity and diversity of the business process.

Young people are aware of the positive and negative images of business and industry in the media. The characterisation of the media as being anti-business was not supported by the findings of the Oxford study, however the manufacturing industry was criticised, with pollution being highlighted. Negative impressions can be supported in curriculum material and the Oxford report found that, despite the enormous progress in this area, there was little awareness of the links between schools and industry. The negativism of the teaching profession manifested itself in industry visits that were used to highlight only the negative factors of manufacturing industry. (*The Formation of Young People's Attitudes Towards Business and Industry*. University of Oxford Department of Educational Studies for Industry in Education and the Design Council. undated)

In 1995, the charity Understanding Industry published a research project by the Centre for Applied Social and Organisational Research at the University of Derby. The project examined the attitudes of 16- to 19-year-olds towards industry and commerce. The study revealed that teenagers had a narrow view of 'industry', associating it with traditional manufacturing and processing. 'It just seems monotonous', said one respondent. Another said, 'you don't get anywhere'. The majority of the 600 respondents shared a negative view of British industry although 78 per cent saw themselves working in 'business'. Not surprisingly, most 16- to 19-year-olds want a job that will be interesting and exciting but these characteristics were not associated with industry. The respondents had a very high level of social awareness but much lower levels of business awareness. Caring professions, for example nursing, fire fighting and teaching were regarded as more important than industrial jobs. Generally, the level of understanding about British industry was poor: the majority of the participating students could not define what the initials CBI (Confederation of British Industry) stand for or name three of Britain's top companies. Sadly, most of the 16- to 19-year-olds said they had not received sufficient careers advice – 56 per cent stated that neither school nor college had prepared them adequately for work.

Careers advice and guidance is provided by both teachers in schools, and careers advisers employed by the Careers Service. Careers education should increase an individual's knowledge, understanding and experience of opportunities in education, training and employment. Careers guidance then helps individuals apply the relevant knowledge, understanding and skills to making decisions. Overall it appears that careers advice is unsatisfactory, providing too little too late for those leaving school.

The Labour Party have proposed a 'jobs highway', using the Internet as a means of making information readily available to young people. School leavers will also receive extensive personal careers advice when they start seeking work and this will be linked to an under-25s task force, using the time and experience of committed local business, education and community leaders. Labour proposes to use the Employment Service to drive their initiative forward across the country. Let us hope that such proposals are effective.

The politicisation of schools

In his book *In Pursuit of Happiness and Good Government*, Charles Murray quotes Alexis de Tocqueville, the 19th century French historian. (De Tocqueville was sent to the USA in 1831 to report on the prison system and returned to publish a penetrating political study *Democracy in America*.)

'The township is the only association so well routed in nature that wherever men assemble it forms itself. Communal society therefore exists among all peoples whatever their customs and laws. Man creates kingdoms and republics, but townships seem to spring directly from the hand of God. It is in the township, the centre of the ordinary business of life, that the desire for esteem and the pursuit of substantial interests ... are concentrated; these passions, so often troublesome elements in society, take on a different character when exercised so close to home, and, in a sense, within the family circle ... Daily duties performed or rights exercised keep municipal life constantly alive. There is a continuous gentle political activity which keeps society on the move without turmoil.'

What the Frenchman says here about the township could equally be said about the school. National education policies, the national curriculum, and our desire for standardisation, have all taken power, independence and innovation away from individual schools. As de Tocqueville goes on to say:

'The difficulty of establishing a township's independence rather augments than diminishes with the increase of enlightenment of nations. A very civilised society finds it hard to tolerate attempts at freedom in a local community; it is disgusted by its numerous blunders and is apt to despair of success before the experiment is finished.'

Similarly, in education in the 1960s, new approaches to teaching involved abandoning techniques that, whilst unfashionable, worked. Phonetics, a learning process using the sounds of letters, is an important building block for learning to read. Many teachers saw phonetics as old-fashioned and didactic, and thought that somehow children would learn to read by a 'look and say' approach, using word recognition. This approach does not appear to have worked and there are still astonishingly high levels of illiteracy in Britain and America today.

Education problems start at the primary level. Half of all primaries are falling below acceptable standards, according to the Chief Inspector of Schools (*The Times* 6 February 1996). Literacy and numeracy problems are widespread. Poor test results for 11-year-olds have highlighted the problem: based on 3,500 inspections, the teaching of reading was described as 'mediocre' or 'poor' in many junior schools. According to the Chief Inspector, there are twice as many good teachers as poor ones, but he estimated that 15,000 were incompetent and should be dismissed if they could not be retrained. Those teaching the four years of junior school, pupils between 7 and 11, often had insufficient knowledge of their subjects. Throughout the primary years, more use should be made of 'whole class' teaching alongside the individual teaching that occupied threequarters of the school day. In 1995, an Ofsted report found that 21 per cent of junior school lessons were unsatisfactory. In most organisations, where such demonstrable shortcomings were evident, detailed performance measurement would be put in place to identify exactly the source of those problems and corrective action taken. However, the National Union of

Teachers criticised plans to publish league tables of performance for 7-year-olds, claiming that such tables would seriously damage standards. Naturally the unions are unwilling to accept any suggestion that teachers themselves can be a major contributor to the problem. Union leaders often blame the curriculum, disruptive children, uncaring parents and limited resources, and it is true that all these things can be contributory factors. However, league tables can provide clear, quality information for parents – of good performance as well as bad.

The British Labour Party's anti-private school policy is likely to increase the difference between the best and the worst schools. The charitable tax status of private schools is likely to be reduced, resulting in an estimated 8 per cent rise in school fees. It will be even harder for parents to be able to afford the best for their children and thus reduce choice. Professor Michael Barber, an educationalist and adviser to Tony Blair, has advocated twinning private and state schools so that, 'Comprehensives would contribute their knowledge of how to get value for money, and their experience of dealing with children from a wide range of backgrounds. Independent schools could contribute in terms of expectations, the pace of lessons and ways of teaching.' New Labour has, however, dropped its 1980s commitment to abolish private schools altogether, perhaps as a result of parental demands for choice.

Ideological dogma that perpetuates low standards in the state sector and stifles new initiatives are as common in the USA as in the UK. Some forward-thinking companies in the USA are setting up satellite schools for their workers' children. When Hewlett-Packard wanted to establish such a school in Santa Rosa, California, the city council objected to the proposal, claiming that the project was 'elitist'. The company agreed to open 20 per cent of the enrolment to non-HP employees, disappointing many staff whose children were on waiting lists. Again local politicians attacked, this time claiming that the school might be hazardous to the environment. Hewlett-Packard eventually won their battle but it was a long, bitter struggle at the expense of the children's education.

We continue to defraud thousands of young people by subjecting them to a substandard and outdated educational programme. As we approach the Millennium we need the courage and political will to test bold new initiatives to find ways of educating all young people to use their abilities to the full.

PART TWO

Making the education system work

Chapter Five
Preparing Pupils for the 21st Century

'Education is the best provision for old age.'
Aristotle (384–322BC)

What do people need to learn? Should broad subjects be taught, such as citizenship, emphasising the individual's rights and obligations in a democratic society? Should the curriculum include the teaching of life skills, to enable us to make the best of our future? What minimum level of attainment should we expect before people are allowed to leave school? What about those skills that will enhance our chances of getting a job and being a productive employee or employer? What about equipping us to cope with the demands of lifelong learning?

Students often say that the school curriculum is irrelevant to their future endeavours: that what they are studying in school seems to have little bearing on what they expect to do in the workplace. The perception that school is not like 'the real world' leads to disinterest and poor pupil performance. Most students believe they will learn work skills on the job. But surely it is possible to adjust the curriculum and change the presentation of material to show its relevance to work, so that students are more likely to be interested and motivated by it.

Rousseau's proposition, after all this time, remains relevant: 'Sound education can never consist of filling a young mind with a large number of facts or phrases that the student does not understand. Rather, sound education progresses in harmony with the stage by stage unfolding of the nature in a child. The process as well as the goal is education for happiness.'

Certainly employment does not always bring happiness, but unemployment is so often accompanied by unhappiness. In fact as many as 50 per cent of those who are unemployed suffer from clinical depression. (Hartley Booth MP *Return Ticket* 1994)

As the renowned educationalist, Elliot Eisner of Stanford University, suggests, vocational training is counter to the position of 'academic rationalism'. Eisner argues that a major function of school is to foster the intellectual growth of the student in those subjects that are most important to study. He also says that 'differentiation of programmes for individuals of different abilities creates a self-fulfilling prophecy that sets limits on aspirations, forecloses one's options in life and provides only a small portion of the total population with the kind of educational repertoire that optimally foster the development of rationality'. In response to this argument I suggest we need more realism, less idealism, in our educational institutions. Schools are failing to meet the needs of significant sectors of society. Failure to provide appropriate educational products for people with different abilities, aptitudes, interests and objectives is to subject the audience to a 'one size fits all' solution which ignores individual needs.

The educationalist Ralph Tyler suggests that curriculum designers should define the educational purpose of the school. Of course there are many purposes in learning. An important one is to equip the student with the means to live a fulfilling and meaningful life. For most people, being employed is an important aspect of attaining that fulfilment. Graduates who cannot find work because of basic skills deficits have not been adequately served by their teachers or their education system.

For too long the 'essentialists', those who see the role of education as the passing on of the great body of knowledge, have held dominion. Their views are often in conflict with 'sociologists' whose perspective emphasises the problems of contemporary society as a key curriculum element. The 'progressive' (and I use the term in the American educationalist sense rather than in its British one with a political connotation) looks to the students' interests and needs. Perhaps we need a new term – the 'vocationalists', who have a new perspective based on providing an education that actually equips a student for work.

An American study by Judith Little looked at the compromises of purpose in vocational training in a three-year study of five high schools. The study found that schools and teachers accommodating an 'academics first' policy compromised both academic and work preparation. Little also discovered that an institutional dichotomy exists between the college-bound and the non-college-bound student. She states that vocational offerings are valued by administrators and councillors only to the extent that they appeal to academically unsuccessful students and relieve some of the burden on the school. The study confirmed the view that the integration of vocational and academic study is far from reformed. (Judith Warren Little, NCRVE, Berkeley CA, 1992)

What initiatives can we establish to improve students' attendance and participation, and to give them a sense of the relevance of their studies? What can teachers do to help their students? Teachers themselves need to understand the standards required by employers. Their knowledge can be developed by involving local companies, inviting managers to speak at their schools and asking parents, who are in employment, to share their experiences. Parents, too, need to be aware of the skills employers require and must influence their local school to provide them, through direct action, participation in school governorship and via parent/teacher associations.

Businesses can provide enriching experiences, by offering 'school to work' preparation, as well as giving assistance to school staff to develop links with local employers. They obviously understand the skills that are likely to be needed at work and through these links with schools can take a more positive role in influencing the education debate. A British initiative, the Business Education Compacts, has shown promise. (Compacts are partnerships between schools and local employers.) By establishing local relationships many of the misunderstandings between teachers and employers have been removed. The result has been improved employment prospects for youngsters from their better understanding both of the work environment and employers' expectations.

Students are often unaware of the vast range of opportunities that exist for them. How do we disseminate this information to broaden the horizons of young people? In Los Angeles, after the horrific riots of 1992, this issue was considered of paramount importance by the Education Task Force of Rebuild LA (RLA). It found that there were many work and training opportunities available but that young people had great difficulty in finding out about them. RLA has now developed a computerised database of training establishments in the inner-city area. Use of the database is free to community organisations and young people who seek specific information about opportunities. If this proves successful the model could be used in other American cities.

Addressing the problem of how young people in Britain find out about opportunities, the broadcaster and writer, Martyn Lewis, compiles a handbook called *Go For It!*. Distributed to every school in Britain, *Go For It!* lists hundreds of organisations with contact addresses, numbers and a brief outline of the services that could be of use to young people. The book, revised annually, has been immensely successful with tens of thousands of copies printed each year. In 1996 Lewis and I established YouthNet – a national information service for young people. The database holds information on a vast range of subjects and is available free of charge over the Internet (http://www.thesite.org.uk).

Citizenship

In the US every school pupil learns about the structure of society and the individual's role and responsibility within it. In Britain we do not teach citizenship, although there is an Institute for Citizenship Studies, founded by Lord Weatherill (Speaker of the House of Commons from 1983 to 1992) to encourage the study of citizenship in schools.

There are important philosophical issues to address when we think about teaching citizenship. For example, should schools teach people to fit into society or teach them to try to improve society? Should emphasis be placed on obedience to the present authorities, loyalty to current forms and traditions, and supporting the *status quo*? Or should such teaching take a revolutionary form and be more concerned with critical analysis, encouraging independence, self-direction, freedom and self-discipline?

In Denmark, it has been decreed that every student leaving secondary school must in their final year complete three challenging self-directed projects related to real world problems with reports to be prepared in three different media. These projects are judged acceptable or not acceptable against high expectations by juries drawn from the wider faculty and community. Some projects are done in teams, but the emphasis throughout is on 'metacurricular' abilities, i.e. the ability to see beyond the narrow confines of the standard curriculum.

Core skills

Education reform is making progress. The definition of core skills continues to get closer to the needs of employers, yet this is only helpful when the skills themselves are being fostered in the student. The British National Curriculum Council agrees on six core skills (very similar to those described in the Education 2000 programme in the USA):

1. Communication
2. Application of number
3. Problem solving
4. Information technology
5. Personal skills
6. A modern language competence.

In 1989 the National Centre for Vocational Qualifications added 'working with others', and 'improving learning and performance' to the list. Three core skills are mandatory at the GNVQ level – communication, numeracy and IT – but none are yet mandatory in A-level courses.

There are calls from employers' organisations to include learning core skills in many qualifications. For example, the Design Council has said, 'As the future prosperity of the UK is primarily dependent upon the ability of our businesses and industry to compete in world markets, it is essential that our education and training service provides the core skills necessary to create a flexible and relevantly educated work force.'

The experience in the USA is that young people's interest in learning falters between the ages of 10 and 12. The conventional wisdom in Britain is that core transferable skills should be part of the post-16 curriculum. Waiting until then means that those most likely to benefit are excluded. ('Transferable skills' are generally regarded as those which will be of use to students regardless of their chosen career path.) Skills such as problem solving, team work and the ability to communicate can, and need, to be taught in most school courses. I hope that we will see core skills become a standard part of the education process in the future, while A-levels and other highly academic courses become the exception. Of course there is no reason why core skills could not be introduced in some form in every A-level course as well.

Another important area in which pupils need to develop expertise is in taking responsibility for a task. Often this is not learned in school, but business considers this a core employment skill. For instance, completing one's school assignments does not have the same significance as being responsible for tasks which directly affect, and are judged by, others. Adolescents commonly vacillate between the desire to take on large responsibilities and the fear of failure. Learning to take decisions and to bear the consequences requires considerable practice. Gradually becoming more responsible should parallel the increase in the competence and confidence of youth. Schools alone can contribute only a minor range of learning experiences for this purpose. Situations that are perceived as real are necessary. In other words, young people must have the opportunity to experience genuine decision-making in business, industry and other work-related environments.

Employment skills

The educational system that furnishes the experiences through which young people learn the things required to participate constructively in our modern, industrialised society includes more than the school. What children experience at home, in their social activities, in the community, in peer groups, in the reading and viewing of films and television, all affect the learning process. From each of these environments young people acquire knowledge and ideas, skills and habits, attitudes and interests, as well as basic values. The school is, of course, an important part of the learning system. School furnishes the opportunity to learn to read, write and compute and to discover and use facts, principles, and ideas that are more accurate, balanced and comprehensive than those provided in most homes. The school also supplements and complements the learning that takes place in other places and provides an important social framework.

The school can also contribute to the development of social skills that are essential to effective work in the service sector. Schools are societies in microcosm, where young people communicate, cooperate, and compete. Many schools appear to contribute positively to the development of the kind of social skills essential to the work place. But the numerous reports of poor performing schools show that a significant number are doing a second-rate job. The 1996 television images of violent pupils at the Ridings School in Yorkshire, where discipline and moderated social behaviour had collapsed, were a reminder of how far some schools are from the ideal environment, i.e. an environment where learning takes place in a supportive and constructive atmosphere.

Business is a highly competitive endeavour. Companies have, for the most part, been transformed over the last 25 years, with increasingly professional management, the introduction of sophisticated computer and communications systems, and global marketing techniques. Modern work practice emphasises cooperation, team work and decentralised decision making. Yet too many schools appear relatively unchanged, persisting in the use of traditional teaching methods, resulting in a stultifying experience for pupils and teachers alike.

A report published in 1989 by the MIT Commission on Industrial Productivity compared the characteristics of a modern corporate environment to the traditional model. Today, in many older companies, work is organised along traditional lines. The emphasis is on mass production with post production quality control. By contrast, more modern – or 'high performance workplaces' as MIT calls them – have flexible production with decentralised decision making and on-line quality control. There is a spirit of worker-management cooperation, more creative remuneration structures and greater demands for thinking and interpersonal skills.

Many traditional subjects can help in the preparation of students for work, but it is important that the work perspective is carefully considered during curriculum design. For example, mathematics problems should reflect real world situations, while science subjects can shift their focus from being a primer for specialisation at a higher education level, to a broader subject coverage for the non-specialist.

In the Adult Performance Level study (referred to in Chapter 2), the authors laid down a set of objectives for functional competency. They said that students should have a goal to develop a level of occupational knowledge which would enable them to secure employment in accordance with their individual needs and interests.

The study recommended that students' specific objectives include:

1. Building an oral and written vocabulary related to occupational knowledge.

2. Identifying sources of information which may lead to employment such as newspapers, magazines, job centres etc.

3. Defining occupational categories in terms of the education and job experience required, and to know minimum requirements of given occupations.

4. To be aware of vocational testing and counselling methods which help prospective employers recognise job interests and qualifications.

5. To understand the differences among commercial employment agencies, government employment agencies and private employers.

6. To prepare for job applications and interviews.

7. To know standards of behaviour for various types of employment.

8. To know attributes and skills which may lead to promotion.

9. To know the financial and legal aspects of employment.

10. To understand aspects of employment other than financial which would affect the individual's satisfaction with a job.

(Norvell Northcutt, *Adult Functional Competency: A Summary*, The University of Texas, Division of Extension. Austin, 1975.)

Employers would be delighted to be able to recruit young people who came prepared with some knowledge of these things. In over 20 years of employing people, I can honestly say that I have never met a school leaver who has any but the most basic understanding of such factors.

Enterprise education programmes

Earlier in the book we have seen how work patterns are changing and that significant numbers of people are becoming self-employed or working for small businesses. In Britain about 40 per cent of people are employed by firms employing less than ten people. The better prepared a school leaver or graduate is for work, the better chance they have of securing employment or successfully entering self-employment and trading viably.

A number of excellent schools programmes have been successful over the years in developing an understanding of the business world, but more still needs to be done. The greater the number of vocational skills acquired within the classroom environment, the better will be the prospects for many young people. Two outstanding initiatives are the American Junior Achievement programme, and the UK's Young Enterprise.

Junior Achievement

Founded in 1916, Junior Achievement (JA) is one of the oldest and largest economics education programmes in America. JA aims to provide young people with a foundation of skills that will make them more employable and encourage a greater understanding of the whole economic process.

In the original Junior Achievement programme students set up a company and trade for a school term. Through hands-on experience and with the help of a business mentor, students learn every aspect of running their company. In the light of the national US mandate for economics education for all school pupils, and the increasing need for high quality educational material for teachers, JA expanded their curriculum dramatically during the 1980s. In 1992, 1.5 million students from kindergarten through to high school participated in a broad range of economics and business programmes.

Young Enterprise

Young Enterprise offers a similar course in Britain. In 1996 the organisation involved almost 40,000 young people in setting up 2,500 companies in 2,000 schools and colleges. Secondary school students set up a business, register for VAT and open a bank account. Each business appoints a board of directors and trades actively for an academic year.

Research done by Young Enterprise shows that the experience of participation is seen as positive by prospective employers and that 'Young Achievers' as they are called, have significantly better prospects of employment. (YE Internal Study 1993.) Kate Orebi Gann at Marks & Spencer specifically highlighted the YE programme as: 'Tremendously helpful; graduates wanting to enter the world of work today not only need to have acquired a level of qualifications, but also to have developed interpersonal skills. Employers are looking for business awareness, communication skills, teamwork and leadership ability, that has been demonstrated in a variety of situations throughout academic and personal life. YE provides a unique context in which students can develop, demonstrate and record their competencies in these vital life skills.'

Besides setting up and running a company, the students are involved in national and pan European competitions and trade fairs. One student commented that 'taking part in YE has made me much more self-confident about myself.' Others value the chance to meet people from other countries as well as putting something really positive on their CVs.

Young Enterprise also runs a programme called Project Business which shows younger pupils how business works. In 1995 more than 2,000 students took the course. The 10-week programme develops business awareness through activities led by a local business volunteer. For Year 10 (14- to 16-year-olds) the course includes nine hours of classroom activities and a business visit. Young people are introduced to the skills they are likely to need in adult life – as producers, consumers, managers of household and business budgets, as employers and citizens. The sessions cover areas such as the market economy, advertising, and personal and business finance. The emphasis is very much on learning by doing, with activities forming the major part of the programme. A follow-up study of the trials of Project Business found that students gained experience of how Britain works, how business works, about the daily economic and business life of their communities, the work of local business people and how to manage their money. Project Business also benefited teachers, and the majority of those that participated felt that their school too had benefited. Teachers particularly welcomed the chance to work with someone outside the teaching profession and to develop links with local business and industry.

Understanding Industry

Founded in 1977, Understanding Industry aims to 'increase knowledge, enhance skills and improve attitudes towards industry and commerce through the delivery of unique and high quality programmes designed to inform, involve and inspire 16- to 19-year-old students'. In 1995 Understanding Industry ran over one thousand courses in schools reaching an estimated 26,000 students. The programme helps to create effective local partnerships between business and education and arrange programmes which demonstrate how companies operate and the ways in which they contribute to the economy. The courses take place in curriculum time and the emphasis is on student participation involving practical experience. Business volunteers are used from 1,300 companies to lead the sessions. Subjects such as an introduction to industry, marketing, design and development, production, finance, personnel, management and small business skills are all covered.

Students who have work experience gain in many ways. Work prospects are improved by the insight gained into work and working habits, and students can learn specific skills, for example working with money, using computers and typing. Teachers also support the view that having some work experience is beneficial in improving students' motivation and maturity. Other reported benefits include heightened sensitivity to other people, a boost to confidence and the acquisition of a broader perspective on life. The downside is that experience of work may reinforce the view of some pupils that school is irrelevant.

Many educators argue that teaching pupils about business or entrepreneurship is inappropriate in school. Others, who are willing to accept the concept, are unsure how to teach it. The Entrepreneurship Education Program, started by Ohio State University, is an interesting example of a staged approach: the university's programme offers a life-long learning challenge to young people who are interested in business and developing their entrepreneurial skills.

The Entrepreneurship Program at Ohio University suggests that there are at least five distinct stages of development in this life-long learning model. It assumes that everyone in the educational system should have the opportunity to learn in the early stages, but that the later stages are targeted at those who choose to become entrepreneurs.

The five stages are these:

Stage 1: The Basic stage, taught in the primary grades, junior high and high school, teaches students various facets of business ownership. They learn about how the economy works and how this results in job opportunities. The expected outcome from this stage is motivation to learn and a sense of individual opportunity.

Stage 2: The Competency Awareness stage, where students learn to speak the language of business as well as see problems from the perspective of a small business owner. Issues covered may include cash flow, linked for example to a traditional maths class, or a sales presentation which is used to develop communications skills.

Stage 3: This stage, named Creative Applications, targets older students. They explore business issues such as planning, enabling them to gain deeper insight than was possible in the earlier stages. A business course of this type is of use not only to those who plan to go into business but in many other professions where business skills may be important – such as running a doctor's practice or a firm of architects. This stage encourages students to create a unique business idea and carry the decision-making process through a complete business plan. It may take place within advanced high school vocational programmes, at two-year colleges where there are special courses and/or associate degree programmes, and at some other colleges and universities. The outcome is for students to learn how it might be possible to become an entrepreneur.

Stage 4: After adults have had time to gain job experience and/or further education, many need special assistance to bring a business idea to fruition. Community education programmes are widely available in vocational schools, community colleges, four-year colleges and universities to provide so-called start-up help. The US Small Business Administration sponsors many of these training programmes.

Stage 5: This is the business growth phase, where the issues of the developing business are explored. Often the entrepreneur does not seek help until it is almost too late. A series of continuing seminars and support groups can help him to recognise potential problems and deal with them in time. Many community colleges and continuing education programmes at universities or colleges offer such seminars and workshops for their business community. They recognise that the best economic development plan is to help the community's existing businesses grow and prosper.

Vocational qualifications

Traditionally, non-academic, vocational classes were only for those not planning to go on to further education. However, today's high-skill job market demands that all high school graduates have both advanced academic knowledge and workplace skills and training. Just as professional careers now demand technical skills and an ability to work in teams, technical careers require an ability to diagnose and analyse problems.

Over the last 50 years there has been a decline in the number of vocational qualifications. The last few years, however, have been encouraging with organisations such as the National Centre for Vocational Qualifications (NCVQ) introducing a wide range of new certifications. The Engineering Training Authority in Britain has encouraged the introduction of greater work place awareness but has noted that improved provision should not be reserved for those who are considered to have a lower academic potential. The battle between academic and vocational education continues. At the 1995 Headmasters' Conference the issue was described as 'thorny' and the view was expressed that vocational subjects might be suitable for some pupils but it was equally proper to use available time for academic subjects. The conference made its anti-business position clear when it was said that 'to make a vocational element mandatory would make (academic) enrichment impossible'.

The Department for Education and Employment has been moving towards giving more significance to vocationally relevant qualifications following the review by Sir Ron Dearing. The Part One GNVQ, introduced in 1995, covers subjects such as manufacturing, health, business, information technology and social care, and allows 14- to 16-year-olds to study for qualifications that develop work relevant skills. In schools where there is a clear vocational element in the school curriculum, there has been very high motivation on the part of students, according to the NCVQ.

Of almost 200 recommendations made to the British government by Sir Ron Dearing, many address the failure of traditional education. He placed strong emphasis on the development of high quality vocational education and a range of new qualifications for low-achievers at entry level below a GCSE grade G. (The grade G at age 16 is equivalent to the standard expected of an average 11-year-old, so is not especially demanding.)

Dearing suggests that society needs to place more emphasis on the key skills of communication, numeracy and information technology and sees these as part of the new national certificates and diplomas. He has also proposed renaming the GNVQ the 'applied A-level'. The editor of *The Times* described the suggestion as a dubious virtue, likening it to the renaming of polytechnics as universities. But polytechnics have always provided excellent vocational educational services – the renaming was to deflect the traditional university's groundless snobbery against vocational education.

National Vocational Qualifications (NVQs) are offered at five levels ranging from Level 1 focusing on very basic skills to Level 5, roughly equivalent to a degree. The qualification is not aimed at a particular age group, rather, at achieving and being able to demonstrate a range of competencies resulting in a pass rather than a grade. The range of subjects available for study is quite remarkable, covering 735 areas and representing the skill competencies of about 86 per cent of the workforce. Since its inception less than a decade ago, one million certificates have been awarded. In one aspect the NVQ has been less successful, in that the qualification has not replaced the plethora of other vocational awards. In 1993-94 there were more than threequarters of a million other qualifications awarded compared to 237,000 NVQs. But the introduction of the NVQ programme has certainly been a step forward in developing and encouraging the study of vocational courses. As with A-levels, there has been some criticism that NVQs are too narrow and don't provide the broad foundation of knowledge necessary for modern employment.

Britain's Labour Party has established 'Target 2000' to ensure that by the age of 18 all young people will have intermediate qualifications, including core skills, by the year 2000. Labour plans to oblige all employers taking on 16- and 17-year-olds to allow time off for training.

The school-to-work transition

Richard Riley, US Secretary for Education said recently, 'Many students just drift through school. Suddenly, when they graduate, they realise they have no idea in the world of how to get a job ... We never make the basic connection between learning, a pay cheque, and some basic career goals. We need to reinvent the American high school to find a way to catch the attention of these young people and help them get a focus in their lives a little earlier.'

The same could be said in Britain. The US has taken bold steps in their school-to-work legislation to develop a more structured approach to the transition process from the closed environment of the school to the open market search for employment. It is worth taking some time to explain the process in the US because it provides a useful template for development in Britain.

On 4 May 1994 President Bill Clinton signed the School-to-Work Opportunities Act. The law provides seed money to states and local partnerships between business, labour, government, education, and community organisations, to develop school-to-work systems. The Act doesn't create a new programme, rather it allows states and their partners to bring together efforts at education reform, worker preparation and economic development, in order to create a system for preparing young people for the high wage, high skill careers of today's and tomorrow's global economy.

School-to-work programmes restructure education so that students improve their academic performance and get 'turned on' to learning. In this way all students are equipped with the knowledge and skills necessary for economic success in the real world. The programme is not intended for the 'non-college-bound'.

Children learn better when they see a purpose to their studies; and cognitive research shows that people learn best by doing – applying their academic lessons to real world activities and situations. By linking schools and workplaces, school-to-work programmes thus improve student motivation and academic performance. The educational experience is also restructured so that students can see how academic subjects relate to the real world. Teachers work together with employers to develop broad-based curricula that help students understand the skills needed in the workplace. Students develop projects and work in teams, much like the modern workplace. Teachers work in teams too to integrate their usually separate disciplines and create projects that are relevant to work and life in the real world.

There are numerous ways in which different subjects can be integrated. For example, in the US, business students learn about the history of Andrew Carnegie and J.P. Morgan in American industry, in conjunction with the mathematical and managerial skills they will need in business. Students hoping to enter nursing learn about genes and atoms, as well as how great authors' illnesses and mental conditions shaped their own pictures of the world. Future artists study not only the art of the past but also learn anatomy and the mathematics that governs perspective and distance.

The US school-to-work initiative builds on the best school restructuring efforts already under way in schools across the country. The role of the teacher is critically important for success, and new demands for cooperation between teachers must be met. Interdisciplinary teams need to show the connections between subjects and to integrate academic lessons with lessons learned in the workplace. Teachers must guide and coach students to learn on their own through projects and problem-based curricula. The business community plays its part too by helping to teach courses in schools and assisting teachers in the planning of those courses to make them relevant.

Student progress is evaluated both by what students know *and* by what they are able to do. The assessments used to measure a student's academic and skill development include portfolios and exhibitions.

In the next stage of the programme, careers guidance staff work towards informing all students of their full range of options – in both higher education and the workplace. The objective is to help students graduate from high school with an awareness and understanding of the full range of options, including four-year college, two-year college, technical training programmes, registered apprenticeship programmes and skilled entry-level work on career paths. Focusing on students' own interests and their relationships with adult mentors provides students with the motivation to learn and a support structure for doing so. Students then study and complete lessons, not to please the teacher or to avoid failing, but because they understand how the material will help them later in life. Ultimately they can see the connection between their classroom lessons and their future careers.

Using federal seed money, states and their partnerships design the school-to-work system that makes the most sense for them. There is no single model. While these systems vary from state to state, each provides every American student with:

1. Relevant Education, allowing students to explore different careers and see what skills are required in their working environment.

2. Skills, obtained from structured training and work-based learning experiences, including the necessary skills for a particular career as demonstrated in a working environment.

3. Valued Credentials, establishing industry-standard benchmarks and developing education and training standards which ensure that proper education is received for each career.

There is no single answer to the question 'what is school-to-work?' It establishes the infrastructure for a system that includes many different aspects; across America, local communities have created their own individual programmes using local legislation to tie together the varied approaches. The School-to-Work Opportunities Act is administered by the National School-to-Work Office, under the joint direction of the US Departments of Labor and Education. As we have seen, the Act encourages educational and career opportunities for all students by creating a framework for business and educational partnerships at both state and local levels. But rather than create yet another new programme, the school-to-work initiative tries to bring together existing models, such as youth apprenticeships and career academies.

Guidelines seek to ensure access for all students, including those who are economically disadvantaged; of diverse racial, ethnic, and cultural backgrounds; students with disabilities; students with limited English proficiency; both low-achieving and academically-talented students; and former students who may have dropped out of school.

The recognition that neither academic nor occupational education alone can provide all students with the skills they need has encouraged the integrated curriculum approach. Modern skills, for example problem-solving, reasoning and interactive learning, are necessary for both further education and high-wage employment. Integrated learning also restores meaning and relevance to the student's experience of schooling, transforming a disjointed series of courses into a cohesive and relevant whole. Integrated learning is also a teaching strategy that more closely matches human cognition than traditional high school class work. Cognitive research shows that students who are the passive recipients of education are usually less able to apply what they have learned in the classroom to other settings.

Integrating school-to-work into the curriculum

When most people hear the word 'curriculum', they visualise school classrooms where students acquire knowledge through a standardised course of study consisting of readings, lectures, written assignments, and perhaps some discussion. The School-to-Work Opportunities Act broadens the meaning of curriculum by calling for integrated learning organised into coherent sequences around broadly conceived career specialisations. Work experience, as well as academic and occupational study, is an assumed element of the integrated school-to-work curriculum.

In the United States, educators, employers, and unions have implemented a variety of approaches to develop this integration. A number of state and local school systems have organised curriculum councils, which bring together interested parties to discuss the options for integrating classroom instruction with work-based learning. (I should perhaps point out that American educators have much more flexibility to develop their curriculum than their British counterparts.)

School administrators can play an important role in encouraging collaboration among teachers from different disciplines. Two or more teachers can work together to coordinate their class instruction, develop materials, and link academic and occupational skills. Teacher collaboration often takes place in curriculum teams formed around an occupational theme.

The development of integrated learning programmes requires an investment of time to enable teachers to examine, experiment, and evaluate alternative approaches. A number of schools give teachers extra preparation time in the summer to work with employers and unions to develop curricula that integrate academic with work-based learning. Experience in the workplace allows teachers to gain a better understanding of the business process and internships with local employers can develop valuable skills.

The Southern Regional Education Board (SREB) in the United States has developed 18 'high-schools-that-work' sites that are serving as 'advanced integration models'. To develop integrated curricula, each site establishes a team of academic and occupational teachers and administrators. Each site also designates a coordinator to provide leadership, represent the team, and complete team reports. The teams have at least 10 hours a month to plan interdisciplinary learning activities, and participate in a one-week summer curriculum development workshop sponsored by SREB. Team members can also attend SREB-sponsored autumn and spring workshops and discussion sessions.

Developers of integrated curricula will find a great variety of approaches and models, ranging from the relatively simple, involving two or three subjects, to the more complex, in which the entire school is restructured. The American programme Jobs for the Future produces a 'tool kit' to help schools establish integrated curricula, suggesting three examples of how this can be done.

1. The coordinated curriculum realigns course work so that instructors in different disciplines teach related topics concurrently, using occupational themes as the organising principle for integrating academic lessons, occupational study, and workplace experience.

2. Project-based learning engages teachers and students in creating projects organised around an occupational or on-the-job issue. This type of approach requires students to apply what they have learned both in the workplace and in school to solve practical problems.

3. A thematic curriculum eliminates the traditional distinctions between disciplines, instead organising learning around questions or problems within themes relating to school and work. Students then address them from the perspectives acquired from both academic (history, science, etc) and workplace learning.

A project approach to curriculum integration can be highly effective. The Trigg County High School in Cadiz, Kentucky, has developed a project in which students design a competitive proposal for construction of a company's corporate headquarters. Using the budget, location and company profile, students develop the proposal from start to finish. Student activities include determination of building specifications based on location and company profile, a title search to ensure that property is available for construction, preparation of working drawings, an environmental impact study, writing the proposal, and the presentation of it to a judging committee. Thus the project incorporates a variety of disciplines: English, in the writing and presentation; science, in conducting the environmental impact study; social studies, in studying the corporation and its requirements; business, in conducting a title search; and technology, in developing floor plans, elevations, schedules, and models.

Curriculum alignment links instruction in one of two ways: first, horizontal alignment, in which teachers within a grade level coordinate instruction across disciplines. The second, called vertical alignment, occurs when learning is connected across grades in order to build cumulative, comprehensive, increasingly complex sequences of learning experiences. Junior Achievement's economic education programme achieves this by building an economic model that becomes increasingly complex over a six-year period. The curriculum starts with the economy of the individual in the student's first year and then progresses through the stages of the family, the town, the state, the nation and finally the world.

Roosevelt Renaissance High School in Portland, Oregon, provides an example of both vertical and horizontal integration. The school created 'career pathway teams' covering a four-year curriculum for each of six distinct pathways. These teams continue to work on integrating basic skills instruction into the pathways. Each of the Roosevelt curricula initially focuses on building a solid foundation of academic skills while instilling responsibility, self-esteem, and work ethics. Teachers incorporate applied learning techniques within reading, writing, and mathematics classes. The relevance of class work is emphasised by constant demonstrations of the connections between school and work. A variety of teaching methods and classroom activities, including hands-on projects and student portfolios, encourages the development of teamwork, problem solving, critical thinking, and communications skills. As students explore career options, the curricula provide career information, planning, and guidance for all students.

In the US occupational high schools and some 'magnet schools' (schools which place special emphasis on academic achievement or on a particular field such as science, designed to attract students from elsewhere in the school district) have made curriculum integration the foundation for school-wide restructuring. Schools that are occupation-orientated often have access to additional resources such as specialised equipment and curricular materials, industry advisory boards, and an established network of work-based learning opportunities.

Career academies (i.e. schools within schools) offer many of the advantages of occupational and magnet schools, yet usually operate on a smaller scale. The typical career academy, which has a team of academic and occupational teachers working with the same students for two or three years, offers a wealth of opportunities for curriculum integration, including work-based learning. Oakland Health and Bioscience Academy exemplifies the school-within-a-school approach to curriculum integration. Integrated curricula in maths, science, English, social studies, and health encourage students to apply the knowledge acquired in one subject to interdisciplinary projects and internships. Portfolio assignments and projects integrate school-based and work-based learning, and academy teachers regularly meet industry supervisors to coordinate school and workplace curricula. In addition, all students are expected to complete practical tasks that engage them as positive agents of change, applying newly acquired academic and technical skills in their own communities.

Whatever combination of strategies a school-to-work system adopts, the school-to-work curriculum by definition must integrate academic and occupational study with work-based learning and work experience.

Misunderstandings about school-to-work education

A common perception is that school-to-work education programmes are designed for the less able or non-college bound. Traditionalists view vocational education as second-rate and for early leavers. This may have been true in the past, but today's job market requires highly skilled entrants with both sound academic achievements *and* workplace skills and training. School-to-work programmes aim to develop an understanding of work and employers' expectations. The objective, as we have seen, is to improve learning through more interesting and relevant experiences that integrate school-based and work-based learning. School-to-work experience is designed to develop young people's competence, confidence, and connections so as to ensure successful careers and citizenship. These skills were cited as most important by large employers such as Marks & Spencer and Grand Met.

Another criticism of the school-to-work concept is that it is unnecessary because secondary schools already prepare pupils for college and careers. But the old 'drill and grill' method of educating young people cannot keep up with the changing demands and opportunities of modern society. We can no longer afford a two-tier educational system, with high-standard academic preparation for some, and low-standard general track or vocational preparation for others. Today's schools must offer all students challenging, relevant courses and worthwhile work-based learning experiences in their communities.

The consequences of the American education system being out of step with the changing nature of work have taken a toll on American business. More than 50 per cent of US employers say they cannot find qualified applicants for entry-level positions. It is estimated that American business spends nearly $30 billion each year training and retraining its workforce. The situation in the UK is no different, only the scale is smaller. Until we fully address the mismatch between what and how students are learning in school and what they will be required to know and do to ensure successful careers, this figure is likely to continue to rise.

It is sometimes said that school-to-work programmes push students into inferior programmes of study with low academic standards that lead to dead-end, low-skill jobs. However, a well-designed school-to-work programme helps to break down the barriers between academic and vocational learning and infuse each with the best aspects of the other – students are expected to meet high academic standards, and academic knowledge is acquired that is not taught in the abstract.

Some educationalists believe that young people won't want to participate in school-to-work programmes. The evidence is quite the opposite. Young people want new learning opportunities and are particularly interested in having a chance to develop vocational skills. According to a recent US Department of Labor survey of 500 American teenagers, 90 per cent of them said they were interested in learning both in school and on the job in the school-to-work way. Two-thirds of high school students want to gain work experience while in school. Three in four teenage workers say their jobs are not preparing them for the careers they want, and 85 per cent of working students say they are learning while working.

Industry tends to support school-to-work partnerships because they represent an investment in important 'human capital', producing highly trained, versatile workers, certified and knowledgeable in all aspects of an industry.

Successful school-to-work programmes

Successful school-to-work programmes reconcile the needs of schools and employers and overcome the barriers to collaboration through developing understanding of the issues affecting both sides. Through regular communication between employers and teachers learning in both settings can be coordinated so that each experience reinforces the other. In the United States, successful programmes have used intermediary organisations – a local chamber of commerce, private industry councils, or a community

-based organisation – to help the partnerships develop and stay together. In Britain there are numerous groups who could offer similar support, including chambers of commerce, local CBI groups and the Business Link network.

Student commitment and enthusiasm will of course increase if they perceive the benefits of school-to-work projects. Young people are concerned about employment prospects, and the knowledge that assistance will be given to find an appropriate job should be a powerful incentive for students to make the additional commitment that learning in a working environment demands.

There are also benefits for the participating companies. Encouraging workers to become involved in youth development activities builds team spirit and a sense of community.

Work-based learning

In the workplace, there are no textbooks with questions to be answered at the back of each chapter. Instead, workers learn by doing, acquiring knowledge as necessary to complete projects. Thus their skills develop through daily use. If we were to align schools with modern workplaces, teaching arrangements would consist of flexible teams of teachers guiding student workers who were empowered to find solutions, not several independent 'bosses' shuffling passive learners according to 45-minute periods. Evaluation would focus on the development of students' critical thinking, problem-solving, ability to communicate, and interpersonal skills, rather than on their ability to memorise and regurgitate information.

Local employers should be encouraged to provide work shadowing opportunities. In this way powerful insights can be gained without significant demands being made on participating business partners. Volunteer work can also be a source of insight into how organisations operate.

In effective school-to-work programmes, employers, workers, and teachers outline the skills necessary for each job, and then work together to help students acquire them. Curricula at school and work are designed to reinforce each other.

Dr Michael Benz of the University of Oregon has reported a study of school-to-work programmes. Oregon State's Youth Transition Program has carried out a comprehensive evaluation of the impact of the school-to-work system on specific student outcomes. This found that participants consistently fared better than non-participants in terms of wages, employment, and productive engagement. The study also found that rural students do as well as non-rural and 'at risk' as well as those not at risk.

Youth development

Who is a successful young person? In the United States, policy makers and practitioners often emphasise the traditional view in answering this question: the successful young person is defined as someone who avoids problem behaviour such as substance abuse, delinquency, and early sexual behaviour, and achieves the traditional benchmarks of high school graduation, stable employment and post-secondary education. The youth development field identifies a third category for success called 'developmental outcomes'. This category involves giving young people a positive sense of self, a sense of connection and commitment to others, and the ability and motivation to succeed in school as well as to participate fully in family and community life. Ultimately, young people who acquire these 'developmental outcomes' are more likely to be deemed successful according to the traditional measures of achievement as well.

Both the school-to-work system and youth development theory share an emphasis on actively preparing youth for adulthood rather than simply preventing their engagement in problem behaviour. The belief is that young people develop by learning actively and in context, and that they need opportunities to interact with and be respected by adults. High expectations of young people should be set and reflected in our own behaviour. For all young people to become contributing adults, school-to-work systems must also incorporate many of the essentials of the youth development perspective.

Emotional support is obviously important during adolescence. Although the strongest potential source of support is the family, young people also benefit from the support of other adults – teachers, relatives and youth workers – who consistently demonstrate acceptance, affirmation, warmth, interest, and a sense of fun. Most of us remember a few cherished people who demonstrated those characteristics in our youth. What power they had to change lives.

Young people achieve more when they are fully involved in social networks, either through their families or on their own. Extended social networks, consisting of relatives, religious counsellors, school teachers, youth workers, neighbours, and other adults, provide significant and strategic support. Our schools could do much more to encourage the development of these networks through community involvement.

To take a specific example from the United States, let us consider Carl, in his second year at high school, who has built a foundation for the transition to work. He attends a career academy that operates within a large comprehensive high school. The close-knit school-within-a-school has strong support and involvement from industrial and post secondary partners. Carl has the same team of teachers for his academy classes, which include English, maths, science and social studies, computer applications and health occupations. Several of the classes are linked with local community colleges as part of a 'Tech Prep' partnership. Carl and his classmates are 'block-scheduled', facilitating special interdisciplinary curriculum, group projects, and field experiences. In addition Carl keeps a portfolio documenting his work. This year, Carl will perform 100 hours of volunteer service in a hospital, earn CPR and first aid certification, attend health career conferences, and frequently go on field trips to health and science facilities. Also he will maintain weekly contact with an adult mentor, who works in either a health care or bio-science profession. As a junior, he will explore careers by rotating through a series of medical and business departments in health care facilities, and he will be trained as a health peer educator. He will have paid internships in the summers following junior and senior years, and during the second term of his senior year. As an intern, he will also keep a journal, attend weekly workplace reflection seminars, and participate in community-based projects.

As a senior, Carl will produce a major health-related project, with teachers and industry partners as his coaches, and complete a portfolio of his work in the academy. After graduation, Carl can enter community college programmes in allied health, biotechnology, nursing, or physical therapy, continue his education at a four-year institution, or get a skilled, entry-level job. 'I feel I am more prepared and more knowledgeable than any of my friends preparing for college. I work in a real hospital, with real patients and real employees. I have hands-on experience ... My job is important and people rely on me to do it well.' (The National School-to-Work Learning & Information Center, Washington DC)

Fort Pierce Central High School – a case study
Performance Based Diploma Program (PBDP) was developed in response to a school dropout crisis. In 1987, Fort Pierce Central High School in St Lucie County, Florida, had a dropout rate of 60 per cent, the highest in

Florida and one of the highest in the country. It was evident that the number of disinterested, disillusioned, and discouraged high school students was increasing. Although many students were of average or above average intelligence, a large proportion were functionally illiterate and had little idea of the responsibilities, demands, and rewards of the world.

The Port St Lucie Chamber of Commerce developed an action plan to tackle the problem. They gave $1000 to the school board to show community commitment to the project and then started recruiting mentors and harnessing local business support. A private industry council was established to involve local business. The council developed a performance contract that made $100,000 available to the county for students proving successful through the programme. A new, performance-based diploma was established to provide personalised learning experiences for each student. Using a non-traditional approach, entrants for the new diploma course were assessed to determine their knowledge and needs. An educational plan was then developed jointly with the student, a counsellor and his or her parents. Academic subjects were studied in a computer lab while a range of vocational experiences included a workplace. Class and work experience scheduling was flexible, as were enrolment and transfer dates. Assessment was ongoing and there was a variety of graduation options.

By June 1994, the performance based diploma had cut the dropout rate to less than two per cent. More than 90 per cent of Fort Pierce graduates now go on to college, enter the military, or take entry-level employment. The school reports significant improvements in attendance, grade point average (test scores), and first-time honour roll students.

Gender career discrimination

In both Britain and the United States there are significant disparities between the earning power of young men and women. These differences are perpetuated by the educational process where teachers and students have lower expectations for women. School-to-work initiatives can be applied to break stereotyped perceptions of career opportunities. Young women making the transition from school to adult life often pursue significantly different paths to those of young men. These differences have economic as well as career implications. In the 1990s in the United States about half of young women aged 16 to 24 work in jobs that pay an average wage of $338 per week, while 60 per cent of young men work in jobs that pay an average wage of $448 per week. This $110 per week wage differential is linked to the different occupations in which women and men are employed and the fact that women are still discriminated against in certain work places. Young women tend to be employed in a narrow range of occupations, in the lower-paying sales and administrative support jobs, while young men are more likely to work in higher-paying machine operator, craft work, and repair jobs. For example, young women aged 16 to 34 represent only one per cent of automobile mechanics, four per cent of airline pilots and navigators, and 10 per cent of electronic technicians, compared with young men in the same age category (Women's Bureau, US Department of Labor).

School-to-work initiatives are attempting to provide young women with access to the same opportunities as young men, particularly in 'non-traditional' occupations where women represent less than 25 per cent of the individuals employed – for example in skilled trades, technology and science occupations. Young women can be helped to develop the skills required for these occupations as well as be shown that these careers are viable alternatives.

There are rapidly expanding career opportunities in high technology, yet such jobs are traditionally dominated by men. These occupations require competency in higher-order maths and science: the participation and achievement of young women in maths and science courses tend to decline as they move through the education system. However recent studies by Ofsted in Britain show girls doing better than boys in all subjects including the sciences due in part to social changes and the increasing number of women in traditionally male-dominated roles.

The importance of parents in school-to-work transition

Parents, the primary shapers of young people's motivation and values, are obviously in a powerful position to convince them of the importance of education and productive work. There is plenty of evidence to show that when parents are involved in their children's schooling, those children are more likely to succeed both at school and at work. As children grow older, the role of the parent inevitably becomes a balancing act between providing support and encouraging independence.

As their children's first teachers, parents have a unique opportunity to provide early career exploration and the basic skills necessary to succeed. As children progress through school, parents can help them learn at home, monitor school assignments, and encourage career-related activities outside the classroom. But traditional attitudes take time to change. Teachers' and parents' expectations for young people will evolve and broaden as school-to-work initiatives develop. They must be reassured that vocational training is not just for the less able, and shown that all levels of employment opportunity can be enhanced through better understanding of career opportunities. The US experience has shown that parents need better information to help their children plan a career. Eighty-three per cent of respondents to a recent survey by the Center on Families, Communities, Schools & Children's Learning, identified information about planning for their child's future college or work as the most important of 19 topics.

Teachers play an important role in encouraging parental involvement. Too often, contact is made only when there are serious behavioural problems rather than as part of a regular process. A strong relationship between parent and teacher can be invaluable in helping pupils select, develop and achieve their educational and career goals.

A recent trend is to sign contracts between parents and teachers. The contracts set out the expectations of both parties and the part they will play in the pupil's development. In Britain, both Labour and Conservative politicians have advocated these written agreements. In the school-to-work context, employers too can be involved in the contractual agreement, setting out their role in the individual's learning process. A benefit of this approach is the development of shared and clear expectations and a foundation for the understanding of broader career possibilities.

Small business in school-to-work partnerships

Small businesses represent a resource of tremendous potential for school-to-work partnerships. The Small Business Administration in the United States reports that in 1992 small business provided 53 per cent of all jobs and created two out of three new jobs. In Britain, a third of all workers are employed in businesses with less than 10 employees. In many communities small businesses are the only employers. These small firms can provide a unique learning environment for young people by providing the chance to see entrepreneurial skills at first hand. In addition, a motivated young person can make a real contribution to the business, heightening the learning experience and student satisfaction.

Several factors help to explain the limited involvement of small businesses in youth development programmes. For example, because small businesses have relatively few employees, each one of them typically performs multiple roles that a larger company would assign to several people. In addition, major employers tend to employ specialised personnel staff with the time to attend partnership meetings in order to develop and administer placements. The urgency of running a business also tends to make small firms more isolated from the school system, less connected with other companies, and less aware of school-to-work initiatives. Thus it is not easy to develop partnerships with small firms. The process takes time and a long term commitment through the development of personal contact. Cultivating these relationships, often through parental introductions, can obviously be helpful in bringing a school and community closer together.

The East San Gabriel Valley Regional Occupational Program (ESGVROP) in Los Angeles, California, offers an example of a successful small business partnership programme. More than 300 businesses are involved in it, ranging from large corporations to small businesses such as veterinary hospitals, real estate offices, and retail stores. In a recent statewide survey of school-to-work transition programmes conducted by the California Educational Research Cooperative, ROPs were found to have a significantly higher involvement of business people and more opportunities for student work experience than high schools, adult schools, or community colleges. Key elements of their approach to building education and business partnerships include using personal contacts and local chambers of commerce.

Helping school dropouts

School dropouts find themselves outside the school support system and unable to benefit from initiatives such as a school-to-work programme. But the process of integrating school and work experience can operate in both directions. Young people who have dropped out should be able to participate in work experience and be encouraged to re-enter the school system.

Young people often leave school for reasons that overwhelm the effectiveness of any 'dropout prevention' programme – such as poor academic achievement, discipline problems, substance abuse, pregnancy, and other family responsibilities. Left to face the demands of work and life on their own, with minimal academic, occupational, or social supports, these youngsters are unlikely to achieve their full potential. They need 'second-chance' programmes as well as prevention efforts. Out-of-school youth may need the opportunities that school-to-work provides even more than in-school youth. Secondary school dropouts, as well as young people who have drifted into poor jobs after school, generally do not develop the same skills and competencies as those still in school.

Dropouts are usually highly sceptical of the education system, and must continually be shown the relevance of what is learned in the classroom to the workplace and to their own future. An effective programme at the Garibaldi School in Mansfield involves regular visits to the school by working managers who describe their businesses and organise regular school trips to their companies. The school fosters a democratic and open approach to learning, welcoming parents back to the school for new educational experiences.

Mentoring can be a powerful way to motivate students. The following case of a Texan student called Olivia illustrates the point. Four years ago, Olivia was on the fast track to trouble. A student at a large, inner-city school in Texas where young people routinely had to pass through metal detectors, Olivia had little time or energy for school. She grew up in a broken home and had been the victim of abuse and violence. Her circle of friends was involved in drugs, petty crime and gang activity. After repeated suspensions, Olivia dropped out part way through her sophomore year. A year later, she moved to Austin and enrolled in James Bowie High School. She hung on, but with no direction or motivation and no plans for what she might do after graduation. Her grade point average was 1.0.

Things turned around for Olivia in her senior year. An attentive counsellor at the school, knowing of Olivia's experience working in restaurants and her love of food preparation, suggested that she enrol in the school's Culinary Arts Catering Program. Once in the programme, Olivia worked in the school's own student-run catering business and participated in structured internships at the University of Texas on-campus catering business and at the Central Market. In addition, she was matched with a mentor, a local chef.

These experiences and the caring relationship with her mentor and her culinary arts teacher helped. Olivia started to believe in herself and found new motivation and drive. She graduated from high school with significantly better grades and began working at a full-service resort and inn as well as at her mentor's restaurant. In the autumn, now 18 years old, encouraged by her mentor Olivia entered a registered apprenticeship programme to become a certified chef. 'I owe my whole life to the programme – and to the support I have received from my mentor.' (The National School-to-Work Learning & Information Center, Washington, DC)

A barrier to the encouragement of young people to return to school is the continued treatment by teachers of young adults as children. Today's 15- to 17-year-olds respond most positively to adult treatment and expectations. Young people who do not continue their education often leave school out of boredom or frustration with the school system. School seems to them to be disconnected from 'real life'. To overcome this problem it is vital to identify young people's strengths and career interests, and then ensure that courses and work placements reflect these interests.

Schools all over the United States are developing new programmes for 'at risk' pupils. The Milwaukee Public School System's Division of Alternative Programs, for example, are designed to support adolescents who have dropped out of school, are behind their peers academically, have high rates of absenteeism, or fit a variety of other at risk characteristics. The public school system operates the 31 alternative schools, each of which contains a school-to-work component. These schools act as 'learning communities', with small class sizes and a specific, occupational, and/or cultural identity. For example, one school offers bilingual classes to assist Hispanic students to adapt to the demands of the workplace. Another school is designed to address the needs of pregnant women and young mothers, by providing extensive social supports not present in the regular educational system. Thus these young women are given the opportunity to return to or stay in school.

Milwaukee's alternative schools are based on the needs of the students. Individual curricula are designed to incorporate the interests and goals of each student. These are then reinforced by substantive work experiences that allow young people to apply the skills learnt in the classroom. Several schools offer half-day academic programmes that provide classroom instruction in the morning and work-based learning experiences in the afternoon. This approach demonstrates to students how school relates to work, fostering improved academic achievement and workplace performance.

UK Careers Service and the transition from school to work

Little attention so far has been given to the role of the Careers Service, which provides an important link between schools, places of further and higher education and employment. The Careers Service in Britain aims to provide impartial advice to its clients on appropriate routes into employment, whether directly from school or into further and higher education. Its clients include adults as well as young people, but its core activity is guidance to school and college students. They have about 7,000 staff of whom 4,000 hold a diploma in careers management. In 1993-94, 1.2 million individual careers guidance interviews were held in schools and colleges.

Despite three significant pronouncements on the future of education in the UK (by the National Commission, the Dearing Report and the

Government White Paper, July 1997) very little attention has been paid to careers advice. Sir Ron Dearing has said: 'Failure to realise the potential of all our young people will undermine our economic performance and quality of life.' Surprisingly, he said nothing about how careers advice should fit into the school curriculum. The earlier report by the National Commission on Education, which was set up by the British Association, said: 'The Commission is convinced that a well structured system of (careers) guidance has potential for helping pupils to make progress: for promoting independent learning by pupils and developing their awareness of the directions they might take in future: and for encouraging the idea of a continuum of learning throughout schooling and beyond. Such support should be an entitlement for all children from primary school onwards.'

A three-year study by Searchlight on Education made two significant discoveries; that there is no certified training programme for teachers who provide career guidance and advice, and there is no comprehensive database of information available either to those in search of employment or those in need of staff. A survey by the National Association of Careers and Guidance Teachers and the Institute of Careers Guidance, published in January 1993, showed that a quarter of secondary schools had no written policy statement for careers education and 70 per cent of those described as 'senior careers teachers' had no professional qualification in careers guidance. More than 10 per cent of schools were providing no careers education at all for fifth-year students.

Many believe it is too early to include career education from the age of 10 or 11 years old, i.e. at the start of secondary education. Conversely, the Confederation of British Industry (CBI), argues for an even earlier start, during the primary stage. Clearly today's school leavers need to be prepared for the likely periods of unemployment they will face throughout their lives and pursue, where possible, those options that give the most flexibility when the inevitable job search begins.

Careers education and guidance in schools is provided by careers teachers. The calibre, expertise and experience of careers teachers varies quite significantly from school to school. A recent Ofsted report found that one third of schools provided good or excellent careers guidance but unfortunately another third had poor provision where the career advice was of limited benefit to students.

The Director of the National Institute of Careers Education and Counselling is aware of the importance of the changes brought about in the workplace by technology and new working practices. 'What we are talking about here is not just about the advice given to young people about the immediate choices ... it is about developing the skills which provide the basis, the foundations, for life-long career development, recognising that there are massive changes taking place in the world of work at the moment ... If individuals are going to cope with these changes they have to have the skills to manage their own careers.'

There has been criticism from employers that careers advice often tends to underrate the work-based route as a post-16 option, that schools are failing to accept the reality that two thirds of school leavers go on to work rather than entering higher education at 18 years of age.

To summarise: the careers service suffers from a lack of coordination, variable quality, poor communication, often out of date information and no national database of available information. What is needed is comprehensive, up-to-date information, easily provided using technology, such as the Internet and CD ROMs. Optic-fibre networks are already transmitting data at speeds unimaginable a few years ago. The super-highways, for example, can transmit the contents of the *Encyclopedia Britannica* from London to Leeds in one second – and transmission speeds are doubling every year. In 1995, according to the DfEE, 2,000 schools had one or more modems and every school had PCs. Facts about job opportunities and those seeking employment could be supplied by individual schools and employers and then this valuable information could be kept on computers, the database maintained by Careers Service staff in local education authorities. Six thousand UK schools already have Internet access according to BT, through their Campus World project. The cost of keeping a comprehensive careers database up-to-date would be remarkably modest – and it could be accessed for a few pounds a month for those schools without Internet access. (Gee, F.C., Weale, R.A., *The Careers Service: Diagnosis and Remedy*. Searchlight on Education 1995)

Young people generally report unfavourably on the careers advice they receive at school. Many feel that advisers just want to ascertain what they want to achieve and then point to subjects and grades needed to reach those goals. Very little effort seems to be made to help young people explore their interests and motivations and to present the options that might be available. Pupils often feel that teachers are adamant that further and higher education is the only acceptable path into working life. (*The Formation of Young People's Attitudes Towards Business and Industry*. University of Oxford Department of Educational Studies for Industry in Education and the Design Council. undated)

Chapter Six
Time for Change

'*Deep down I am very optimistic because I see it is a time of great opportunity for a lot of people who never thought that they could actually make a difference to the world.*'
Charles Handy, *Rethinking the Future*

At work employers use teams to manage most processes, yet in British schools teamwork, in academic subjects, is rarely evident. Individuals work on a task and if they consult their colleagues their so-called 'cheating' is punished. There is also a stark contrast between the availability and application of technology in school and office. In the industrialised nations virtually every business has up-to-date computer terminals linked through networks and able to operate powerful software. Yet despite the enormous investment in Britain's education system over the last 15 years, many classrooms struggle with a limited number of obsolete computers and poor software, used sporadically by often untrained teachers.

In the next century pupils may learn efficiently without classrooms, or teachers, or even schools. There is evidence that appropriate technology can play an important part in the education process: it can certainly help many of the poor quality, unenthusiastic teachers who are in the profession today. Why would a parent want to send a child to a school where there is violence, disruptive behaviour, drug abuse and little evidence of quality teaching? Surely home schooling, or some form of cooperative project, using the latest technology of the Internet and satellite television, will do a better job? In America one million families have taken the home schooling approach and the numbers are growing each year. In Britain there is already a dramatic increase in the number of people trying home teaching; as technology provides the tools, it seems likely that even more parents will turn away from schools and have a go at teaching their children themselves. The unionised tenure system that guarantees a place for the worst teachers and drains the well dry so that there is nothing left to attract better motivated, younger teachers, is failing to provide the quality of learning experience many parents expect for their children.

The originators of career education were clear in their recognition that the classroom is as large as the community. The natural tendency of some teachers, however, is to do what they have always done – reduce the outside world to what can be put into a book or a lesson plan or what can emanate from the teacher. This principle of abstracting the outside and bringing it in, based on the presumption that what exists in the present can best be understood through observation of the past, is counter to the value of hands-on experience – which is the preferred teaching method of most post-school learning experiences, such as learning to drive, fly an aeroplane or operate a computer.

What can we learn from the classrooms of Asia? In some respects East Asia has been tremendously successful in raising its standards of education. In the 1995 World Competitiveness Report, Singapore and Taiwan were placed respectively first and third on their educational system's ability to meet the needs of a competitive economy. In countries such as Taiwan, Singapore and South Korea, the priority is to raise the standards for all pupils rather than the wealthy or the clever élite. The governments of these countries have invested substantially in primary education.

The success of Asian Americans in winning places at the best universities in the USA has been so significant that schools such as Harvard and the University of California are debating the need to balance student numbers. According to *The Economist* (21 September 1996) over 10 per cent of American doctoral degrees in science and engineering went to Asian students in 1996.

The fact that Asian families are deeply committed to their children's education may be a factor in this marked difference in performance. Also the Asian school year is longer, exams are more frequent and there is a pervasive belief that everyone can succeed. It is worth noting that high expectations are a factor that crops up repeatedly when successful schools in America and Britain are studied. Asian schools appear to be better at giving remedial tuition to those who fall behind and parents are even given a report each day on their child's progress. Teachers are more respected and better paid than in the West.

Alternative models for learning institutions

Should we look for radical solutions to the failure of our education system or incremental changes? Lewis Perelman's book on educational reform, *School's Out*, states his position clearly: 'The classroom and teacher have as much place in tomorrow's learning enterprise as the horse and buggy have in modern transportation … in the 21st century learning is in and school is out.' Perelman's book develops the view that archaic teaching practices cannot survive the impact of new technological developments that make knowledge instantly available.

The overriding issue facing educators today is how to cope with the transformation wrought by communication-age learning systems. If schools are to become significantly better, they must make significant changes. 'Schooling' must be replaced by 'learning systems' based on a flexible, pupil-centred approach where computers allow the development of bespoke products to meet individual needs. At present, pupils attend school for six hours a day five days a week for about 28 weeks a year, in a building called school. Teachers control pupils by sitting them at small desks and utilise sets of textbooks and measured time on tasks to 'instruct'. They 'evaluate' the results by the amount of completed homework and the scores on memory tests. I doubt such a system will survive the first decade of the 21st century.

American educationalist and philosopher F. M. Esfandiary has an optimistic vision of future education: 'The future of education is glorious – though it has nothing to do with schools and colleges. Education is bursting out of the schooling system. School is a feudal industrial concept, and is obsolete and unworkable. School systems must develop into communication centres. They must cut down on their industrial rituals, grades, hierarchy, competitiveness. Rather they must foster a love of learning. Unfortunately the present system is not fostering a love of learning, in fact we are strengthening the industrial concept.' (National Association of Secondary School Principles. Bulletin Vol 73, No 514, February 1989 reproduced in *Education Now,* Winter 1996)

Education Now, a non-profit-making educational charity in Britain, suggests that the desired education system places 'an emphasis on personalised education and learner-managed learning with the general aim of promoting an education system for the development of flexible, adaptable and confident people rather than a school system devoted to uniformity and the production of rigid, regressive and fatalistic people.' (Education Now Statement of Purpose) In addition it is stated: 'There should be a focus on the uniqueness of individuals, on their learning experience and their many and varied learning styles. Education should be in human scale settings including home-based education, small schools, mini schools and schools within schools and flexi-learning. To bring out the full potential of the learner we need to recognise that students themselves have the ability to make both rational and intuitive choices about their education. To create the appropriate learning environment we need to encourage schools to be democratic and cooperative places of learning.'

Roland Meighan of Education Now describes three models of educational establishments: the 'authoritarian', the 'autonomous' and the 'democratic'. In the 'autonomous' style, decisions about learning are made by the individual learners. Each one manages and takes responsibility for his or her own learning programmes. Individuals may seek advice or look for ideas about what to learn and how to learn it by research or consulting with others. In the 'democratic' view, Meighan describes the learners as a group that have the power to make some, most or even all the key decisions, since power is shared and not appropriated in advance by a minority of one or more. Democratic countries might be expected to favour this approach but in fact such educational practices are rare.

	Authoritarian	*Autonomous*	*Democratic*
Discipline	learning to obey the rules	self discipline	democratic discipline by working cooperatively to agreed rules
Knowledge	information contained in traditional subjects	repertoire of learning and research skills to deal with new ideas	the skills and information needed by the group to maintain and develop its learning
Learning	listening to subject experts and reading their books	self directed and personal research to gain experience, information or skills	activity agreed by the group to gain experience, information or skills working together or reporting back
Teaching	formal instruction by trained or approved adults	self teaching, teachers are there to teach you how to teach yourself	any activity, including instruction, that the group judges will lead to effective learning

	Authoritarian	*Autonomous*	*Democratic*
Parents	expected to be admiring spectators	part of the team supporting the learner's growth	part of the resource available as partners in the learning group
Resources	subject textbooks, subject teachers trained in mass instructional methods	first hand experiences as basis for personal research	anything appropriate to the group's research and learning including people, places and experiences
Location	central place where experts (teachers) can be assembled cheaply	anywhere useful or interesting	anywhere the group can meet to pursue effective learning
Organisation	classes arranged for whole class instruction	often individual learning stations, flexible to manage many learning tasks	commonly in groups where democratic dialogue and cooperative learning can take place
Assessment	tests of how pupils can repeat the subjects	often self-assessment using tests devised by the learner as appropriate	as appropriate for the situation
Aims	to produce mini-academic subject experts	to produce people with confidence and skills to manage their own learning through life	to produce people with the confidence and skill to manage their life-long learning within a democratic culture

	Authoritarian	*Autonomous*	*Democratic*
Power	in the hands of an appointed individual	devolved to individuals who are morally responsible for the exercise of their autonomy	shared in the group who are responsible individually and collectively

(A Sociology of Educating 3rd Ed. Roland Meighan and Iram Siraji-Blatchford.)

Authoritarian, autonomous and democratic structures are all prevalent in our society, yet few schools are run on anything other than purely authoritarian lines. People schooled under one system are handicapped in modern society. Carl Rogers in *Freedom to Learn* in the 1980s noted that democracy and its values are scorned and despised in school systems. 'Students do not participate in choosing the goals, the curriculum, or the manner of working. These things are chosen for the students. Students have no part in the choice of teaching personnel, nor any voice in educational policy. Likewise the teachers often have no choice in choosing their administrators ... All this in striking contrast to all the teaching about the virtues of democracy, the importance of the "free world", and the like.' The political practices of the school stand in the most striking contrast to what is taught. While being taught that freedom and responsibility are the glorious features of our democracy, students are experiencing powerlessness, as well as having almost no opportunity to exercise choice or carry responsibility.

People need flexibility to cope with change and adaptability must be a priority in learning. The present system based on uniformity is, therefore, counter productive. Society is making progress in realising that life-long learning is essential but too many pupils still see education as a one-off experience to be endured between five and 16 years old. Unless schools change the way they teach and how they manage the learning process, society will continue to pay the price through unemployment and reduced industrial competitiveness.

Private sector funding for education

Dr James Tooley of the Institute of Economic Affairs and Manchester University has questioned whether schooling needs to be provided by the state at all. In a recent book, *Education Without the State* (IEA Education and Training Unit 1996), Tooley cites an example of funding without provision; Britain has social security, but we manage without state food shops. 'One justification for state intervention in education is that, without it, there would not be educational opportunities for all. However, the majority of people would not need state intervention for funding or provision of educational opportunities. Intervention would at most be required for a minority in need of financial support.' He supports his conclusions with historical evidence from Victorian England and Wales, and from more recent experience around the world, where educational entrepreneurs have stepped in to provide opportunities when state education has failed.

Although most schools are not run for profit, a group called Nord Anglia has successfully built up a chain of 20 schools that it runs efficiently and profitably. Nord Anglia improves its acquisitions through economies of scale on everything from textbooks to legal services, and revamps the curriculum to make better use of teachers' time.

In the USA, companies are increasingly contributing to local school programmes for their workers. The more progressive are even starting schools for their own staff. Miami-based American Bankers Insurance Group, operating in Dade County, Florida, built a school in their 84-acre grounds. The group has 1,600 employees and in 1996 the company school had 225 children attending from kindergarten to fifth grade. The company considers the project a good investment, helping them to attract and retain desirable employees who want a good education for their children. The facts support the argument. Staff turnover generally is 13 per cent in the company but only 5 per cent for employees with children at the school. The company estimates that in 1996 it saved almost $500,000 dollars from the project. In first grade reading tests the school scored in the 74th percentile, compared with the 48th percentile for regular Dade County schools. In second grade, the results were even more impressive – American Bankers' children scored at the 88th percentile compared with the county schools at 39th, the national average being scored at the median (50th percentile).

Other similar projects include Barnett Banks Inc., Miami Beach's Mount Sinai Medical Center, and Miami International Airport, where a total of $700,000 has been spent on building a school for 104 employees' children.

Despite the generally destructive unionisation of the state schools in America, the unions have supported the satellite programme because it adds money to public education. (*Forbes Magazine*, 9 September 1996, Nina Munk)

A substantive project in Pennsylvania, however, has been bitterly opposed by the unions, who fear that their monopolistic stranglehold on the state system will be undercut. The state's Charter School Program allows parents and community leaders to design and operate schools free of most state rules and regulations. So far, 30 schools have been created and hundreds more are on the drawing-board. These new schools are showing great promise by significantly improving student performance. While not opting out entirely from the state system, the Charter programme illustrates that freedom and independence in general result in better performance for pupils and value for money for society.

Ideas from America

In the United States, where the breakdown of the inner cities and consequent educational problems are more acute, many other interesting ideas are developing. 'Mindless schools', as the American academic, Theodore Sizer, calls schools, are at the heart of the problem. The factory-like environment of the high school, where students are pushed every 50 minutes from one classroom to the next more closely resembles an assembly line in a factory than a forum where ideas can be exchanged. Teachers are forced to be impersonal and focus more on maintaining discipline than on exciting any interest in their subject.

In a 1994 article in *Business Week*, Sizer set out a series of key principles for school reform. He suggested that educators should have the simple goal of helping people learn to think rather than digest facts, and that time should be spent on mastering a few essential skills and areas of knowledge. Sizer believes that schools should stress values that society considers important such as trust, decency and meeting high standards without anxiety, and that teachers should act as coaches not lecturers. (T. Sizer *Mandate to Mend Schools*, *Business Week* 10 January 1994)

Sizer's 'coalition schools', recently helped with a $50 million grant from the American philanthropist Walter Annenberg, take a refreshing approach to school structure. For example, a team of five or six teachers from various subjects take responsibility for 120 children. This allows bonds to form between the pupil and the teacher helping to reduce the dropout level and the sense of abandonment that many students feel. Subjects become connected, more akin to the real world, and students produce projects that demonstrate learning by developing and defending a portfolio of finished work.

For example, students at Broadmoor Junior High in Pekin, Illinois, recently learned about probability theory by building a mock casino. The students were divided into groups and each group calculated the odds for its casino games. Pupils designed and constructed the mock casino, created advertisements and posters, and gave a presentation on its merits. This example shows the way in which teachers can think differently about the process of learning to make it more interesting and useful to the student who will soon seek employment. At the Pekin school the Principal reported that test results were up, and discipline problems down by 80 per cent. Such changes are not easy for teachers who are used to closing the classroom door and delivering a monologue. (Another school in Louisville, Kentucky, which adopted a similar approach, found that the percentage of students going into higher education increased from 20 per cent to 40 per cent.)

In a class where the material being taught is too difficult for some students, those struggling will tend to misbehave – a manifestation of the frustration they feel. The same holds true when the material is too simple, and boredom sets in. This mismatching is called 'outside the zone of learning'. By sorting pupils by ability rather than the traditional measure of age, we will have narrower zones of learning in a class and hence better learning taking place for more students. This more rational approach would move pupils forward based on mastery of a particular subject rather than on age. I envisage classes where a 14-year-old could be working alongside a 12-year-old or a student who was 17, bound together in that class because they each shared a similar level of understanding of the subject. Teaching would be easier and more productive to those of matched ability rather than matched age. Far narrower extremes of comprehension would be found than in today's typical class.

The Prime Minister Tony Blair apparently supports this idea, '... The revolution in business ... will, over time, take place in education too. We will move away from a system that assumes every child of a particular age moves at the same pace in every subject, and develop a system directed to the particular talents and interests of every pupil.' (Quoted by Michael Barber in *The Guardian* 30 Jan 1996)

Don Glines, the director of the Educational Futures Project and former director of the Wilson Campus School, one of the most innovative schools in America, suggests that society has three choices for the education system of the next century. We can retain the present school system, change it or develop a completely new one. If people believe that the present system is failing in its tasks, the second or third choice are the options. There have however been numerous attempts to change over the last 30 years yet we are still doing a very poor job for large groups of young people. Don Glines is a futurist: he sees the only real option as a new system. (Don Glines *Creating Educational Futures*; 1995, Michigan. McNaughton and Gunn)

The importance of excellence in teaching

There is widespread agreement that excellent teachers achieve excellent results despite limitations of resources or other 'excuses' for poor performance. In the book *Twenty Teachers* common themes emerge. Excellent teachers are 'enablers' who help others do good work and extend pupils' powers. They relate to students as human beings and see each other as equals in human terms even though not necessarily so in knowledge. School is seen as a place which should be characterised by civility within an atmosphere that fosters intellectual and emotional growth. Learning should be exciting and enjoyable: coercion is seen as crippling to the learning process and paralysing to thought. All the teachers identified treated their students with familiarity and affection: 'These teachers don't expect learners to be objective or subjective, but both, not only learning from their own experience and ideas but from setting up a conversation between the two and listening to it.' (*Twenty Teachers* MacRoroie, Ken, Oxford University Press, 1 May 1987)

Interestingly, there is little evidence to link increased funding with better pupil performance. Research by Hanushek at the University of Rochester looked at broad trends in the relationship between the two. In the US real spending per student has almost doubled since the 1970s, but scores on the Scholastic Aptitude Test (used for college entrance and the National Assessment of Educational Progress) have not improved during the same period. Hanushek's study surveyed a cross-section of research on students, teachers and educational achievement. Teacher/student ratios were found to make no significant difference to educational outcome either.

It is misleading to focus entirely on poor performance. Many schools have inspired teachers and consistently provide an outstanding educational experience for their pupils. In 1996, the Chief Inspector of Schools in Britain commended a number of schools for excellent teaching. He found that of the top 32 secondary schools, 22 were grammar schools. (Independent schools were left out of the awards.) One in three grammar schools was said to be outstanding compared to one in 50 state comprehensives. More than half the top schools are single sex, 10 of them girls-only while eight were all boys. Of the outstanding secondary schools, 13 are grant maintained. The schools were chosen because they offered a 'rounded development' with exceptional out-of-hours activities, and entered at least 95 per cent of pupils for GCSEs. On average they achieved a points-score equivalent to at least nine GCSE grade C passes each.

To blame socio-economic factors for failure is false as the success, for example, of Sudbourne Primary School in Lambeth shows. Sudbourne is situated just a mile from one of the worst schools seen by the inspectors, Mostyn Gardens, where every subject apart from music was sub-standard. Sudbourne has a 'calm and greatly admired' head teacher, a caring atmosphere and enthusiasm for books amongst its pupils. The school puts pupils in sets according to ability in reading and mathematics, and encourages children to recite their times tables.

Creating the right learning atmosphere

Many educationalists agree that people learn best when they are self-motivated and take responsibility for their own lives; when they feel comfortable in their surroundings; when teachers and learners alike value, trust, respect and listen to each other; and when education is seen as a life-long process. The least constructive learning environment is where these factors are reversed, i.e. where pupils feel frightened, bored and frustrated, and consequently their learning capacity is severely reduced.

Traditional education has always been about instruction, something one person gives to another, usually allied with discipline. And when the media report alarmingly poor performance in schools, the rallying cry goes out for more discipline – that is, imposed discipline, rather than self-discipline. Successful educators know from their research, and the rest of us know intuitively, that real learning takes place through discovery and interest in the subject within a framework of self-discipline. As Lewis Perelman points out in his book *Schools Out*, the focus for learning should be on an action that is 'done by' not 'done to' the participant.

Classroom behaviour, or the lack of it, is a common problem in those schools that have the poorest education record. Most people would agree that strong discipline breeds good results. The schools that have excellent educational outcomes have established an atmosphere where learning can take place. But discipline should support learning, not stifle it.

Student motivation, and thus behaviour, can be improved by using a simple token reward system. This approach is helping teachers achieve impressive results. Bebington High School in the Wirral, for example, has been using such a programme for two years. When a new head teacher took over the school three years ago he found low-level disruption was seriously affecting some classes. The effects of putting in the new approach have doubled the pass rate of five A to C grade GCSEs from 11 per cent to 23 per cent. The idea is to reward children for desired behaviour and penalise them for unwanted behaviour. The school has established a set of classroom rules which are agreed with pupils and may be discussed with parents. These rules include, for example, arriving on time for lessons, entering the classroom quietly, remaining in your seat unless asked to move and coming to lessons properly equipped. The rules are clearly displayed in classrooms together with the rewards and punishments. Bob Burns, the headmaster of Bebington High, has commented: 'Everybody knows that it is up to them to make a choice about their behaviour. No time is wasted by the teacher in explaining why sanctions or rewards are imposed. This means that the lesson time is used for learning and teaching, not dealing with the disruption. One of the first effects was that teachers were under less strain, and had to prepare more work as the children were getting through much more.' (*The Times* 10 November 1995)

Malbank School in Nantwich, Cheshire, is another highly successful school. In 1996 it beat private schools such as Stowe and Haileybury in A-level rankings, yet it is a state comprehensive drawing pupils from areas with severe economic problems. Nearly threequarters of Malbank's 149 A-level candidates gained four passes and 12 won five or six A grades. Even less able students do well, with a remarkably low dropout rate. The head teacher, Allan Kettleday, has built a reputation for running a happy and disciplined school where the teachers have high expectations of their pupils. In 1977 Malbank changed from a grammar school to a comprehensive and it is the traditional values that have been retained that appear to have at least in part been responsible for the school's achievements.

Of course, change takes time. In the case of the discipline system at Bebington High it took six months of preparation to train teachers, adopt the scheme, develop the rules and decide on the consequences.

Clearly a disciplined learning environment is essential for a successful school, but what about other factors? For example, does class size affect learning? This is a controversial area and academic opinion differs. Classes of 12 to 15 pupils are ideal in my view. This size allows discussion but the teacher can also spend time helping those who are struggling while maintaining the interest of the leaders or the laggards. The Office for

Standards in Education (Ofsted) has found no evidence to indicate that large classes mean lower standards. In fact, Ofsted has identified that in large classes pupils often do better than in smaller ones, citing information from the high-achieving classrooms of East Asia where class size often means 40 or more pupils. However, this can be a misleading conclusion since schools in East Asia have a much longer school year and quite different learning environments to most British schools. A study in the US of 7,000 pupils in 79 schools has shown that younger children in smaller classes will outperform those in larger classes. The research, conducted in Tennessee, showed that pupils between the ages of five and eight years old in classes ranging from 13 to 17 pupils made better progress in reading and mathematics than children in classes with up to 25 pupils.

In 1996 Governor Pete Wilson of California announced plans to spend $971m on reducing class sizes for five- to eight-year-olds. Each class with 20 or less pupils receives $19,500 and schools had until February 1997 to meet the targets. The biggest problem was finding enough teachers: ultimately the state had to find 26,000 new teachers, even though it only licenses 5,000 each year. The massive spend assumes that smaller class sizes will improve learning i.e. that more resources will make the difference. But by international standards California is already generously funded and any failure may be linked to other issues, such as the 100 languages spoken in California's schools or the lack of curriculum and testing standards.

Currently about a million primary-school pupils in England are taught in classes of more than 30 pupils and some classes are as large as 40 or more. More research is required to improve our understanding of the impact of such factors.

The structure of the school day may also affect the efficacy of the learning process. Learning capacity drops in the afternoon – as anyone who has had to give a talk after lunch knows! Perhaps students should tackle more intellectually challenging material in the morning and use afternoon classes for activities that are participatory. Modern teaching materials and visual aids, contextual learning, hands-on experience, computerised systems – all have a role to play in improving the efficiency of the teaching process.

City Technology Colleges

City Technology Colleges (CTCs), are not business schools but an inspired new approach to vocational education. By breaking the traditional mould of school management, curriculum, and finance, CTCs have demonstrated that there can be dramatic improvements in results for even the most disadvantaged. These colleges are new institutions, initially funded by a significant donation from a company and then run by a management board. Fifteen CTCs exist today. The initial CTC programme, founded in 1987, was considered so successful that a second tier of colleges was established. Existing schools were given the chance to convert to technology college (TC) status and so far 151 have joined. CTCs put special emphasis on the skills that are required in our technological age. Pupils enter at the age of 11 and have a high quality vocationally orientated education.

The CTCs' mission statement sums up their objectives: 'To promote an educational culture which is scientific and technological, vocational and international. Up to the age of 16, in addition to teaching the sound and broad educational foundation of the National Curriculum, Colleges will enhance the acquisition of the practical, scientific, technological, mathematical and communications skills needed by the manufacturing and service industries of our country. Beyond the age of 16, Colleges will aim to increase specialisation in those areas. This will ensure that young people will be both well educated and technologically skilled, ready and able to progress into employment, further training or higher education according to their individual abilities, aptitudes and ambitions.'

In 1996 there were over 300,000 school children attending the original 15 CTCs, the 151 new technology colleges and a similar number of affiliated schools. The CTC Trust is funded through an innovative combination of private sector sponsorship and government grant. The colleges have proved to be extremely popular, with three times as many applicants as there are places.

The CTCs deliver all the subjects of the National Curriculum with additional emphasis on maths, science and technology. They are sponsored by industry and commerce and seek to maintain and develop close links with local employers. Although many schools would claim the same, CTCs' founders clearly state that they seek to develop the enterprise, self-reliance and sense of responsibility young people need for adult life and work. By offering a wide variety of course options at age 16, CTCs encourage most of their students to remain in full-time education after 16, the minimum school leaving age. Interestingly, many of the CTCs have a longer school day and a longer school year than average. It should be noted that the original 15 CTCs are independent schools but charge no fees.

The second tier Technology Colleges receive financial support from their sponsors of £100,000, given in cash or kind. This sum is then matched by the DfEE providing £200,000 to pay for the initial purchase of equipment required to support this type of school. Technology Colleges then continue to be maintained schools and receive their annual funding in the normal way. Over and above this, TCs are eligible to receive an additional annual revenue of £100 per pupil per year, linked to annual performance achievement targets set by the DfEE. This additional funding reflects the extra cost associated with operating a technology-intensive curriculum.

Curriculum development has been an important part of the contribution made by the CTC movement. Projects undertaken in the last few years have included the development of keyboard skills, ELOQUENT (an EC-funded project for the development of interactive multi-media vocational language learning), distance learning and the Bradford Business Scheme, a whole curriculum business education.

Contextual learning

The application of contextual learning in American classrooms was first proposed by John Dewey (1859-1952). Dewey, an American philosopher and educator, was a leading exponent of philosophical pragmatism and rejected traditional methods of teaching by rote in favour of a broad-based system of practical experience. He advocated a curriculum and teaching methodology tied to the child's experiences and interests, and deplored the separation of education into mind and body, and of school programmes into academic and occupational tracks. Today the school-to-work movement has become one of the strongest voices raised in support of learning based on the principle that students should interact directly with real experiences.

'Learning in context' is so obvious a notion that the average person might tend to dismiss its importance. Anyone who has ever endured the first day in a new job or started a new hobby or sport recognises that often frustrating confrontation, between a human mind's knowledge and skills, and a new set of cognitive, social, physical, or mechanical demands. Contextual learning is learning that occurs in close relationship with actual experience. Such terms as experiential learning, real-world education, active learning, and learner-centred instruction, have all been used to mean similar ideas.

John Abbott of Education 2000 has said: 'The task is to get more students out into the community and more involved in their learning, if we want a learning society. The mistake is to think of learning as a school-based activity, rather than one of life itself. There was plenty of learning before schools were around. Most of the people who flocked to the Globe Theatre to enjoy a Shakespearean play could neither read nor write. Even in

1830, when English inventiveness and enterprise led the world, the median level of schooling was two years. But people learned the practical and intuitive skills they needed through community life and apprenticeships; they worked collaboratively on tasks that made sense to them, and took responsibility for their work. Living, working and learning were interdependent.' (Education 2000 Bulletin)

Lauren Resnick offered a cogent summary of the differences between contextual learning and traditional education in her 1987 presidential address to the American Educational Research Association: 'Social versus individual learning, learning shaped by tools versus learning independent of tools, learning engaged with objects versus learning dependent upon symbols, and learning that is situation-specific versus theoretical learning. Cognitive research, in expanding our understanding of how people learn, continues to demonstrate that schools, as traditionally organised, violate all that we understand about how people learn and apply what they learn to new situations.'

Various strands of research thus contribute to the contextual learning synthesis. One important strand is the research on adult literacy, which finds that literacy education should build on experiences and contexts– such as the workplace – familiar to adults. Ethnographic studies of people performing their jobs have led some researchers to advocate that work preparation should recognise the social aspects of work, and the need students have to experience and reflect on what is happening in order to learn. Other cognitive psychologists have argued that schools are not teaching the thinking skills most required in high-performance workplaces, and they look to contextual learning approaches as a remedy. Derived from this line of research, the concept of the cognitive apprenticeship adapts the traditional apprenticeship model for acquiring physical skills to the acquisition of cognitive skills.

The common sense aspects of contextual learning leave the concept at risk of careless implementation. Simply placing a student in a 'real-world' environment does not guarantee a learning experience. Effective contextual learning results from a complex interaction of teaching methods, content, situation, and timing. The ideas of contextual learning are closely allied to the conceptual foundations of school-to-work programmes that emphasise the relevance of course content. For school, community, and workplace partners, contextual learning means agreeing to a shared vision of a learning programme's goals, whom it should serve, and what strategies it should use to achieve those goals. For educators, adopting contextual learning requires time-consuming and far-reaching changes in practice related to curriculum, instruction, assessment, linkages with workplaces and other areas such as staff development, school organisation, and communication.

Contextual learning requires new approaches in three areas: curriculum, instruction, and assessment. Traditional disciplines have to be adapted to teach material in meaningful contexts and the artificial distinctions between occupational and academic studies need to be eliminated. When the teacher is no longer the dispenser of wisdom and the textbook is not the basis for lesson plans, completely new structures have to be developed. And new assessments must be used to help students, teachers, and parents better understand how students learn once rote learning and textbook mastery are abandoned.

Contextual learning requires a complete reorganisation of the school timetable. Secondary schools typically follow a traditional curriculum, most often divided into 45-minute periods. Teachers usually teach within their disciplines, behind closed doors in isolated classrooms. Contextual learning, however, demands that teachers plan programmes, observe work settings, learn in workplaces, and collaborate with employers and businesses and other organisations where students will be placed for internships or paid work. These are complex and sensitive issues that stir much passion in the educational reform debate.

The Rindge School of Technical Arts (RSTA) in Massachusetts is an example of a successful contextual learning project. RSTA is one of seven 'houses' that make up the campus of Cambridge Rindge and Latin School. RSTA has worked with the university faculty, businesses, and community partnerships in order to develop workplace experiences for students. For example, 11th-grade and 12th-grade students work with Polaroid employees in areas such as instrumentation, electronics, and planning for two-and-a-half-hour shifts for which they earn wages. Students also write weekly summaries of their work and make presentations to Polaroid staff. To prepare for teaching careers, other students enter an internship programme with Lesley College, spending three mornings a week at the college, two mornings in elementary schools, and the rest of the day at RSTA taking classes.

Memory: does it matter?

Society is resistant to educational reform. Traditionalists look back to dimly remembered ideas of their own school days where the emphasis was on memory and repetition. They decry change, whether it be the use of calculators in maths or the development of modular A-levels. But change there must be. Today we need pupils who understand how knowledge can be applied. Tests for progress in a subject should concentrate on understanding, not on memory. Simply put, there is just too much to remember. It is far more productive to teach pupils how to think about information rather than to store a few random facts. Society is being suffocated by the torrent of information and it is increasingly difficult to be well-informed about many things. There is a wealth of available information.

By the year 2000, the *Financial Times* estimates that 500 million people will be on the Internet. Probably every pupil in the industrialised world will have easy access. Today, for about £2 per week plus the cost of a local call, the Internet gives instant searchable information on an estimated 200 million pages – a figure doubling each year. Fortunately the increased processing power and low price of technology are helping us manage the torrent of information. We can harness the enormous power of computers to sift and search for the answers to our questions. The skill of 21st-century workers will be to define the right questions, not remember the answers, and to understand where and how to search for the knowledge they require. The basic processes of thinking, deciding and learning will always be human skills to be cultivated and developed, but the storage of information is best left to machines that do the job more efficiently.

Modern technology allows students to access information almost instantly and information in quantity that was unimaginable 15 years ago. Teachers face the challenge of showing students how to limit their enquiries, the opposite of the traditional approach where pupils were encouraged to undertake the widest possible searches. Technology extends the learning process; it does not dull the mind or cause our thought processes to atrophy but enhances man's abilities. Modern PC programmes utilise software that is extraordinarily powerful, yet demands commitment from the user to master these complex tools and to apply that power to the learning process. School students need to learn how to use these machines, how to work through instruction manuals and help buttons on their computer screens so that they can best harness the processing power of low-cost technology. The computer industry is learning how to teach people to use their products efficiently using electronic tutorials that take the new user through a series of lessons in an interesting and entertaining way. The demanding consumer will not tolerate badly written software, yet most of us have suffered for years from poor teaching materials at school where years may be taken to learn what could have been taught in months if efficient methods had been used.

As Perelman says in *Schools Out*, 'if learning is in everything, everywhere, how do we confine learning to the box of a classroom? We can't. Then what's the point of having schools at all? There isn't any.' And perhaps the only justification for schools will not be the socialisation, which for many pupils is probably harmful anyway, but we may find the only reason we have schools is that parents are too busy working themselves to teach their own children, even though they would make a better job of it. In effect our schools have become day care centres.

Successful schools

The most successful schools create challenging learning experiences for all students. These schools set high expectations, develop challenging lessons and consider alternative models for students and teachers to work together. Successful schools chart progress with a range of assessments to find qualities and achievement in all pupils. The managers in these schools build a culture that supports and develops staff cooperation and participation in decision-making. They find ways for teachers and other staff to collaborate on significant changes needed in the school and actively seek ways to organise resources, and time and space to increase staff collaboration. Ultimately, there is a sense of camaraderie, a belief that all teachers can work together as a team. Parents and the local community are also tied in to the learning process. Pupils are praised, supported and their environment is safe.

Interestingly, schools that are successful have often found ways of becoming independent of their local district's directives and remote or worse oppressive management style. The schools have a sense of 'ownership' and administration is seen as a help, not a power source. Its role is to enable both teachers and pupils to be the best that they can. Numerous successful schools confirm the critical importance of parents and the home and school link.

Common themes emerge time and again in schools that work. I have seen this in visits to schools both in the UK and the US and in the evidence of numerous case histories. Leadership seems essential for a school to do better than the average. For example, in the innovative atmosphere of the Garibaldi School in Mansfield, where Bob Salisbury's leadership overcame political and union opposition to his ideas. (See next page.) Another example is Selly Park Girls in Birmingham, a once troubled school with an 'appalling academic record' which faced closure in 1986. English was the second language for 80 per cent of Selly Park's pupils and the school was housed in shabby buildings. When a new head teacher reorganised staff and transformed the atmosphere by persuading councillors that the largely Muslim intake needed a girls' school, the results were improvements in both enrolment and examination passes. In 1997, about 30 per cent of girls achieved five A to C grade passes at GCSE, compared to a shocking two per cent a decade earlier. The new head teacher motivated and inspired staff and involved parents by inculcating a winning spirit. This positive 'can do' leadership approach makes a significant difference to a school's performance.

The world's largest accounting and consultancy firm, Arthur Andersen & Co, has a model with four management strategies that are constantly emphasised. According to Arthur Andersen, a successful organisation: focuses on customers, energises the employees, manages by facts, and constantly seeks to improve the processes. Translating these four strategies to the school environment they would be:

'Focus on customers' – focus on pupils' needs and parents' expectations.

'Energise our people' – motivate staff.

'Manage by facts' – develop information systems that give you the facts so you really know how people are doing.

'Improve the process' – constantly review how the school teaches and operates to ensure ongoing improvement.

Garibaldi School – A Case Study

The Garibaldi School has 900 pupils aged 11 to 18 years old and serves the mining community of Forest Town outside Mansfield in Nottinghamshire. In the 1990s the village had 16 per cent unemployment and only 4 per cent of the parents have a professional background. The headmaster, Bob Salisbury, is a cheerful, engaging man with great enthusiasm. He told me that he joined the school's staff seven years ago in 1988. One of Salisbury's first tasks was to set five areas of competence for his pupils.

1. Global outlook – all pupils should have a global outlook particularly towards Europe.

2. Communication – pupils should develop communications skills and self-confidence. Salisbury describes this process as the ability to present yourself in the most positive way and the school uses the performing arts to help students develop communication skills.

3. Enterprise and innovation – the school runs numerous projects to help

pupils develop business awareness skills. For example, Garibaldi School forges links with local employers and invites businesses to use the school premises. Pupils are encouraged to think creatively and the school walls are lined with pictures of 'winning students'.

4. Flexibility – this recognises the need to adapt to change through life-long learning. For example, the school encourages adults to return to school as pupils to continue their education. During a school tour I met a mother in a sixth-form class – back at school after raising her children, she was studying for her first A-level. Her fellow pupils were delighted to work with their older classmate and the teacher found the presence of a mature student brought a stimulating and positive challenge to the teaching job.

5. Information technology – all school leavers are expected to have strong IT skills and technology awareness before graduating. In just seven years the number of computers per pupil (my comments on the limitations of this measure are discussed earlier) has risen from one per 87 pupils to one per five.

Clearly there has been a fundamental cultural change at the school. Radical ideas can't be adapted if the atmosphere is wrong, 'you can preach customer care but it doesn't happen without the right culture', said Salisbury. This is even harder if the current culture is punitive. 'It is essential that we see pupils as students – people who want to learn – rather than as children. Discipline in the school is based on mutual dignity and respect.' He draws a clear distinction between friendliness and softness and touring the school one gets a strong impression of a disciplined but relaxed and positive learning environment.

Salisbury's approach to transforming the school involved organisational changes. First he removed all assistant heads and heads of house and adjusted numerous roles. His intention was to cut out those teachers who were involved purely in administration rather than in teaching. A mini 'Ofsted' review group was set up in the school to examine existing practices and find new approaches. The results – dramatic increases in test scores and one of the lowest staffing costs in the county. Staff responsibility was increased and the new title of 'curriculum adviser' was used.

In modern business parlance, the school has customer focus. Salisbury commented: 'The customers are the whole community, parents, teachers, industry, neighbours and, of course, the students.' One neighbour had complained about some students, so Salisbury invited him in for a tour of the school. The complainant, a reclusive concert pianist, was so impressed with the music facilities that he now acts as a volunteer teacher. This sort of innovative approach seems to permeate every element of the school. For example, the maths department was asked to analyse the truancy statistics. Results revealed that pupil truancy occurred almost always in either June or at Christmas. By restructuring the school timetable and activities during these two periods, the reduction in truancy has been dramatic.

This analytical approach is now being extended to explore which teachers get the best results within each department. In those areas where performance was very poor, such as maths, with only three per cent of pupils achieving A to C GCSE passes, new and better qualified teachers were the answer. The results prove the decision was right with test scores at 30 per cent and increasing.

Close parent communication and involvement is also important. At Garibaldi they place great emphasis on parent contact.

Business management techniques in schools
School management and staff motivation involves many aspects of the process of running a complex organisation. High levels of absenteeism are indications of a lack of commitment in any organisation. School is no different. One report found that in some schools, teacher absenteeism was double that of the pupils equalling, in many cases, to more than two weeks in the short academic year. Motivational techniques from business can work well. For example, at Garibaldi there are regular awards not just for the pupils but also for staff. Pens, radios, T-shirts and other popular items have been used to reward hard workers. Many award gifts are donated by supporters of the school and although the gifts in themselves may be modest, the very act of recognising effort has proved a powerful motivator. As one head teacher told me, 'I have worked for 25 years in schools and I can't remember anyone ever saying thank you.'

John Abbott of Education 2000, a UK charity that promotes new educational ideas, offers a reason for this Victorian factory approach. In an interview Abbott was asked, 'Why is it too much to expect that education will help produce self-confident, self-sufficient learners?'

Abbott responded: 'We want them to, of course. But we should understand how against the grain that expectation will be. The system of universal education was set up in the nineteenth century to meet the demands of factory-based work for people with the basic skills and attitudes appropriate to a manufacturing economy – that is, people who could follow directions and perform relatively straightforward, repetitive tasks in a reliable manner. Schools, even colleges, were then organised around a factory model, with separate courses, departments, credits, tests, all in sequence. In the model, learning is seen as an abstract activity, separate from the everyday context, and as heavily dependent on the teacher, who imparts information and routine skills, aided by text books.'

Professor Charles Handy, one of the great organisational thinkers of the 20th century, has written many important books about organisations and more recently about work, society and philosophy. In March 1993 Handy delivered a speech titled, 'Thinking differently about education'. Handy said: 'We have got to stop thinking of our students as products. I once did a study of schools as organisations. I said that the perfect model for the school was a factory, the only trouble was that the students were not the workers but the products – raw material going through various processes, stamped, inspected for quality, with only certified goods going out. What we fail to do is recycle the rejects. What an exciting thing it is to see schools where the students are actually treated as workers, not the products, where they work in groups, solving problems.'

Chapter Seven

Technology and Education: the IT advantage

'Imagination is more important than knowledge in our modern and constantly changing world.'
Albert Einstein (1879–1955)

Professor Steve Molyneaux of the University of Wolverhampton wrote in *Multi Media* (June 1996): 'Pupils must leave school able to read, write, calculate, communicate and work in teams, use technology, recognise right from wrong and know how to learn. This should be our national priority.' Unfortunately this is not what is happening. Britain's school system is structured to produce an educational élite but not structured to produce the type of 'knowledge workers' operating in teams that modern business needs. Professor Molyneaux continued: 'Issues surrounding teacher training, in-service training, staff development and the management of classroom technology remain unresolved.'

John Abbott of Education 2000 has said: 'Technology is on a collision course with conventional education systems. Schools and colleges for generations have been instruction and teacher centred: but the essence of the emerging technologies is discovery, the empowerment of the human mind to learn spontaneously, and collaboratively.'

President Clinton in his 1996 State of the Union Address declared: 'In our schools, every classroom in America must be connected to the information superhighway, with computers and good software, and well-trained teachers. We are working with the telecommunications industry, educators and parents to connect 20 per cent of California's classrooms this spring, and every classroom and every library in the entire United States by the year 2000. I ask Congress to support this educational technology initiative so that we can make sure this national partnership succeeds.' The President's education challenge is based on four key ideas:

1. Modern computers and learning devices will be accessible to every student.

2. Classrooms will be connected to one another and to the outside world.

3. Educational software will be an integral part of the curriculum – and as engaging as the best video game.

4. Teachers will be ready to use and teach with technology.

Society is in the midst of another revolution. Whatever we call it, the information revolution, the technology revolution, or the digital revolution, the fact remains that new high-technology tools are rapidly changing the way people work, the way pupils are taught, and the way in which we learn. In short, technology is revolutionising people's lives, society, and the world. Those who choose to sleep through this revolution will wake to a different world, where they have been left behind.

A fascinating learning phenomenon has occurred over the last decade. Computer users have demonstrated a remarkable revolution in self-teaching. Tens of millions of people have learned to use complex programmes, such as Microsoft Word or the spreadsheet software Excel, with little or no formal training. In fact, since 1980, an estimated 60 to 100 million Americans have learned to use their computers without a classroom teacher in sight. They have not had their work marked or been forced to attend classes. Rather they just read the often difficult manuals and with hours of study have managed to master the required techniques. Clearly technology is intriguing, and when people can learn at their own pace and perceive real benefits from their efforts they are highly motivated. Most people are willing and able to undertake complex learning projects, however long ago they left school and whatever their level of academic achievement.

The growth in the use of technology in both home and office is quite staggering. According to the *Wall Street Journal* (June 1995) 30 million households worldwide use computers on a regular basis. In the USA, 500,000 families join computer networks each month and 10,000 computer CD-ROMs are purchased each week. This growth rate is likely to continue for the next few years. By the year 2003, as many as 43 per cent of Europe's 153 million households with television will also have PCs. Almost all of these PCs will be equipped with a CD-ROM drive that holds the equivalent of 650 paperback books on each disc. (*Time Magazine*, Special Issue June 1995). In America there are already 150 million e-mail addresses and more mail transmits electronically (e-mail) than regular mail through the US post office. Computers are now linked together in offices and schools through Local Area Networks (LANs) and these are expected to grow by 500 per cent in the next five years. Cisco, the Californian company that produces much of the Internet and network technology, has grown in 12 years to sales of $8 billion and a market capitalisation of $56 billion – significantly larger than General Motors. These new businesses illustrate the remarkable pace of change and take up of new technology.

The statistics for technology in households in the UK are equally astonishing. According to a study by Times Mirror Publishing of 4,000 households in July 1994, 31 per cent had a PC and 46 per cent of teenagers had a PC. The study found that 1 in 10 of British households had a modem and with the rapid expansion of Internet access the figure will have increased substantially since then. A *Newsweek* magazine report in 1994 also supported these figures, estimating 150 million PCs worldwide. Of these, 60 million are running Windows software. It is hardly surprising that America's richest man, Bill Gates, made his fortune in computer software. There are about as many computers as cars sold each year, 34 million in 1995. (IEEE Spectrum. Egil Juliussen. Small Computers)

An estimated 80 per cent of all salaried workers will work at a video display terminal by the year 2000. (Hard Test for Soft Products. SIGCHI Bulletin Jan. 1995) The implications of these technological developments for educators and those involved in curriculum design are monumental, yet the statistics of growth are in stark contrast to the apparent low level of teachers' technical literacy.

Britain is well placed to benefit from Internet technologies, with highly developed academic information superhighways called JANET and SuperJANET. JANET is the UK national research network of 200 higher education institutions and gives Internet access. SuperJANET currently networks 60 higher education institutions and is used for distance learning, group collaboration and remote access to information, teaching and expertise, using a high speed optic fibre network.

Although teachers seem slow to adopt new technology, America's parents are motivated to make significant investments in computers. An American Learning Household Survey found that over 80 per cent of intended family household PC buyers in its study cited 'children's education' as the primary reason for purchase, relegating 'work at home' and 'home financial applications' to a distant 40 per cent level. The survey also found that children's use of the PC is shifting away from games and towards more complex uses of the computer as an information access tool.

The US government actively encourages the use of technology in schools with a broad range of support programmes: 'New information technologies provide an opportunity to help all children meet high academic standards ... Meeting high standards means helping all students acquire the knowledge, skills and habits of mind they will need to get good jobs, be good citizens and live good lives in a global community.' (Interagency Technology Task Force. US Department of Education. March 1995.)

While technology is not a panacea for all educational ills, today's technologies are essential tools of the teaching trade. To use these tools well, teachers need an understanding of the technologies' potential, opportunities to apply them, training and support, and also time to experiment. Using technology can change the way teachers teach. Some teachers use it in traditional 'teacher-centred' ways, such as drill and practice for mastery of basic skills, or to supplement teacher-controlled activities. Others use it to support more student-centred approaches to instruction, so that students can conduct their own scientific inquiries and engage in collaborative activities while the teacher assumes the role of facilitator. Teachers who fall into the latter group are among the most enthusiastic technology users, because technology is particularly suited to support this kind of instruction.

For many pupils, IT can provide a safe and non-threatening environment for learning. The computer is patient and does not expose a child to humiliation in front of his peers. Slower students can take the necessary time to absorb material that might otherwise hold up a class and learners with short attention spans or memory difficulties can consolidate material in a productive way. Presentation standards are greatly improved through the use of standard software packages. Going back and checking material is also much easier; clarification and appropriate reinforcement are essential features of educational software.

The effect of technology on motivation is powerful. Often the lack of basic skills prevents children from making progress and can deny them access to some areas of the curriculum. By applying computer-aided learning, children who find writing difficult can be encouraged to express themselves on a word processor without the problems they have been experiencing using a pen. Young writers become much more adventurous, knowing that they can avoid the time-consuming and frustrating experience of recopying. (NCET, Information Technology Report 1994)

Technology can expand hugely opportunities for home education. More than 200,000 students graduate each year from the British Open University, an electronic learning system using broadcast television channels. Innovative universities are offering degrees over the Internet, so why not the whole school curriculum? Satellite television channels in their thousands are constantly beamed to earth, 90 per cent of homes have videotape machines and home PCs are selling in their millions. In the USA, the Office of Technology Assessment found that distance learning had spread from only 10 states in 1987 to 'virtually' 50 states by 1989.

Perelman in *Schools Out* gives many examples of how technology is having an impact on our view of teaching organisations. The National Technological University, an electronic graduate engineering school with no campus and no full-time faculty, beams its 12,000 hours of courses by satellite from its Fort Collins, Colorado, headquarters to over 5,000 engineers. Students are not on campus, but in video classrooms at work sites in scores of subscribing organisations scattered all over the United States. Leading faculties at more than 40 participating universities nationwide provide NTU's telecourses. Students, who are usually employed engineers pursuing further education and professional development, can attend courses anywhere a satellite dish can be installed: and all this at a fraction of the cost of a traditional college course.

Distance learning is already a part of today's learning environment: it is not some futuristic dream. Heriot Watt University in Scotland, for example, has 25,000 students studying for an MBA by a distance learning programme. Since an estimated 40 per cent of American workers do some form of teleworking, the idea of teleschooling is not unrealistic. Distance learning provides numerous benefits, for example saving time commuting and reducing the need for expensive office accommodation. In a *Wall Street Journal* article entitled 'How to communicate in your bathrobe', Edward Segal describes how the California telecommunications company, Pacific Bell (which has a turnover of $8.7 billion and 65,000 employees) launched a pilot programme in the mid-1980s, in which one hundred employees were equipped with portable computers and high speed data links from their homes to determine the benefits of telecommuting. The project was so successful that the company decided to offer it to all employees on a continuing basis. Today, nearly 2,000 employees across California, ranging from financial management staff to engineering and planning personnel, spend between 20 per cent and 100 per cent of their working week at home.

We live in an information age. Students, whether in primary, secondary or post-16 education, will live in a world where the main source of information is through a computer screen. Unlike any previous generation, today's younger generation have the opportunity to communicate with people and organisations on a global scale. The range of learning materials to which they have access is almost unimaginable.

Nick Tate, the UK government's chief curriculum adviser, has expressed a concern common to many traditionalists. He warns of the danger of schools setting too much store by the use of computers at the expense of basic literacy. The image of young people using computers for 'mindless games' is widely held by those unfamiliar with the power of technology as an efficient learning aid. This lack of understanding of how computers can be used effectively to improve literacy will diminish as younger, more technically competent teachers enter the profession.

CBET (computer-based education and training) has yet to deliver radical changes in educational performance but the situation is starting to change as new technologies begin making their way into schools and training centres. The dramatic growth in the use of CD-ROM drives, computers linked through local area networks with Internet connections, multimedia and interactive software is fuelling a new wave of better teaching tools. This generation of technology promises more than just an improvement in educational productivity; it may deliver a qualitative change in the nature of learning itself.

A novel technology programme in Vista High School in Bakersfield, California, shows an innovative approach to teaching pupils about computers. 'Build me, keep me' is a 15-week course during which high school students build their own computer from scratch. At the end of the course they can keep the machine. The project, founded by Henkels, a Philadelphia company, started because the company could not hire enough trained school leavers to work in computer production. So far, Vista High School has produced 500 machines and teachers report that students have been highly motivated and learned a great deal about how the computers work and how to fix them when they don't.

New approaches to educating workers and students are arriving just in time in the view of many experts. The changing nature of companies and the work they do, especially with large scale downsizing and the shift to an information-based economy, is requiring workers to be more flexible and better trained, especially in the use of technology. Businesses require schools to turn out students with a different set of skills from those emphasised in the past. Employers are using new technologies to educate workers and they expect schools to adopt similarly efficient methods. There is an echo of a new way of thinking in education theory: instead of the one-way information flow typified by broadcast television or a teacher addressing a group of passive students, new techniques, such as the Internet, are two-way, collaborative and interdisciplinary. The penetration of technology into the classroom dramatically redefines established teacher-pupil relationships. Teachers change from omniscient leaders into tour guides for the information superhighway. Instructional materials evolve from rigid textbooks into customisable software. Information becomes more accessible, users pick and choose what they want, and everyone becomes a creator. According to R. Wayne Oler, CEO of Thomson Publishing's education group, 'Education on demand, in homes and on the job, will be far bigger business than entertainment on demand.'

An exciting development is the use of 'virtual reality' (VR) programmes. VR is a graphical system on a computer that is responsive to the user's actions, and operates in real time. Learners can enter and interactively explore virtual (3D) representations of real or imaginary worlds, using a computer mouse device to navigate. For example, pupils can travel around a fictional city, move around buildings, explore space or any other environment programmed into the computer. Uses in a curriculum might include pupils in a history class exploring a virtual Greek villa and examining objects within it. A student at Sheffield's Hallam University is currently working on such a project. In geography, VR allows a student to fly over terrain and stop and examine features from different perspectives. VR is increasingly applied to design and product development and an awareness of the technology will obviously assist pupils in their preparation for such work.

British schools have invested an estimated £200 million in computers since 1987 (*Sunday Times*, 26 May 1996) and retailers such as Tesco and Asda have launched fund-raising schemes to provide schools with computers. With an annual spend of £32 per pupil on information technology (IT), Britain invests more than most European countries and even Japan. Even this level of funding is far from producing the impact that society needs.

According to Tim Denning of Keele University, in a study of 3,400 teachers and pupils, many staff were wary of computers, did not know how to operate the technology and used computers for simplistic tasks or not at all. He found that more than half the teachers said they were interested in using computers in class but 70 per cent said they used them infrequently. Another study found more than 50 per cent of 11-year-olds never used computers in subjects such as mathematics, science and English and, remarkably, 20 per cent said they had never used computers. In the same study 80 per cent of first-year undergraduates said they had not used computers at school. (Margaret Cox, King's College, London)

Often, middle-aged and older teachers, trained to use paper, pencils and blackboards find the use of the computer intimidating and confusing and an estimated three out of four seldom use them in lessons. The problems of application don't just relate to a teacher's willingness to master new teaching aids. St William's Primary School in Norwich is not untypical. The head teacher, Michael Garratt, has said that 540 pupils share 19 computers but that some of the computers are 12 years old. The ratio of pupils to computers is regularly cited in government studies, but on its own the statistic is unhelpful, because the age and power of a machine has a dramatic impact on its utility.

In the US in 1995 spending on educational technology proportionately far exceeded the UK's budget. According to the Washington DC based Software Publishers' Association, $2.4 billion was invested in that year alone. In a July 1994 report it was stated that more than half the schools in America used computers in almost every discipline and 99 per cent of schools had at least one computer. Unfortunately only one third of schools have more than one computer for every 10 students – the US national average is one computer per 12 students. It is difficult to know the level of US technology spending in higher education but a report from IBM Academic Consulting estimated institutional spending at $6 billion in 1994 and over the last 15 years schools and academic institutions have spent $70 billion.

The common thread linking American schools, colleges and companies is that all are facing budget pressures and are looking for ways to improve the return on investment. Education and industry are using similar technologies to address similar problems because there is ample evidence that appropriate use of technology can boost retention rates, reduce boredom and misbehaviour, and, in many cases, cut costs. A summary of 133 studies found that educational technology clearly boosted student achievement, improved attitudes and self-esteem and enhanced student-teacher relationships. (SPA's Report on the Effectiveness of Technology in Schools 1990-1994)

Computer-aided learning brings many benefits. For example, pupils learning in a large group are often afraid to speak out because they fear appearing foolish if they give the wrong answer. However, the computer avoids this problem, guiding each learner efficiently to the correct answer or repeating the material that needs further study. Computers thus act as personal mentors, or built-in experts, and are available on demand whenever the student needs them. This makes it cost-effective to return to individual instruction along the traditional model of the apprenticeship, because teachers are relieved of the burden of supplying all the information. Today, computers provide apprenticeships in numerous fields such as flight simulation, military combat and surgery.

Computer games, often derided as debilitating, can provide stimulating learning experiences. Learning should be fun and when it is, we learn more. Computer games are making an impact in some schools. *Where in the World is Carmen Sandiego?* is a popular product that teaches geography and involves chasing a spy around the world. The programme has sold in millions and has been so effective that vast quantities of bootleg copies are said to be circulating in American schools. *Reader Rabbit*, another popular software product, has also sold millions of copies and teaches four- and five-year-olds to read in a fast and entertaining way. There are thousands of innovative educational programmes on the market to help pupils command an enormous range of material. The tools for our schoolchildren to succeed are available today and there is no excuse for the present level of under-achievement and low pupil performance. About 60 per cent of British 11-year-olds are below standard in mathematics and English – an inexcusable situation in this technological age. It is not a question of funding, because funding for education has never been higher in real terms. Britain is spending thousands of pounds per pupil to give the majority a substandard learning experience. If any business treated their customers as many of our schools treat pupils they would be bust, and rightly so.

The new technologies that are making the biggest impact in training and education are networks and multimedia. Networks include the local link-up of computers Local Area Networks (LANs) and Wide Area Networks (WANs), such as the on-line services like the Internet or Compuserve. WANs will probably have the greatest impact, allowing students all over the world to share learning experiences. These technologies, like word processing in the office, will become part of the normal education process.

The irreversible impact of technology will eventually revolutionise the way we educate but the revolution may be slow in coming. Over the last 40 years massive telephone networks have been installed across the globe, school television has been in use for 30 years and the video recorder for 20 years. Computer sales are in the hundreds of millions and satellites beam down hundreds of channels of video – yet the impact on schools has been minimal. With modern teaching technologies almost anyone can learn anything.

Computers have an important role to play in other aspects of teaching. The preparation of materials, notes, slides and diagrams are easier to produce on computer and often of better quality than handwritten material. Using desktop presentation, complex ideas can be more easily explained and the teacher can spend more time on explaining information rather than merely conveying it.

Internet

One of the most powerful and recent phenomena is the Internet. The 'net' started in the United States in the early 1970s as a military and scientific network linking large computers and allowing users to exchange information using a common language. The network grew steadily, adding more and more computer centres and international institutions. The most dramatic change has occurred in the last couple of years. The Internet has opened up to allow home computer users and commercial firms to use the network for a very small cost. The number of Internet users is estimated to be about 60 million worldwide and about 500,000 new users join each month.

The Internet is defined as a network of networks, linking millions of computers and users around the world. Connection, usually through a local service provider for a few pounds a month, gives access to a world of free information sources linking the users to universities, libraries, commerce, government agencies, museums and galleries across the world. Internet also allows people to make contact with individuals in almost every country. People can send letters, photographs and chat on-line for the price of a local telephone call and even listen to hundreds of radio stations and watch television.

How will the Internet affect our education systems and ultimately our prospects for international competitiveness, full employment and the many other expectations we have for society? I would not wish to laud the Internet as some all-powerful solution to the challenges that all developed nations face: however the Internet is a powerful mechanism that signals a revolution in knowledge systems. It may have a more significant impact than any change since the industrial revolution.

In the US, AT&T, the telephone company, plans to spend $150 million to help 110,000 public and private elementary and secondary schools get on-line with links to the Internet, by the year 2000: the largest amount the company has spent on education. It is a proposal similar to one made by Prime Minister Tony Blair before coming into office, in which he pledged that British Telecom would link up every school, library and hospital in the UK. AT&T are also addressing the issues so often voiced about the difficulties of using the on-line software, claiming that they have developed technology that is easy to use for teachers and effective in helping students learn.

The Internet allows students to learn about science in exciting and innovative ways by taking part in live, interactive projects. In Maya Quest '96, US students in grades 4 to 12 rode along with a wired bicycle expedition to explore ancient Mayan ruins. Similarly, a NASA project, 'Live from the Hubble Space Telescope', donated three valuable Hubble orbits to students, allowing them to observe a celestial body of their choosing. The annual JASON Project expedition uses a combination of live two-way video broadcasts and Internet-based curriculum activities to engage school students in exploring underwater conditions in the coastal marine habitats of southern Florida. 'Science and the Environment' is a free news-clipping service for high school students and teachers that publishes articles on various environmental issues. The stories are selected and summarised from more than 500 sources, including newspapers, magazines, research journals, and specialised environmental publications. The service aims to supplement the environmental curriculum with up-to-date information.

In North Reading, Massachusetts, students use the Internet as a means of assessing authoritative sources. Says Tom Hashem, a maths teacher: 'It gives them access to timely information they couldn't find in the local library.' One high school class, studying an Amazonian tribe, joined an anthropological list server and contacted ethnographers who were experts about the tribe. When they got contradictory responses, Dr Maryanne Wolfe, their teacher, said that it taught students that informed sources sometimes disagree. 'Students begin to learn the need to dig into the background and perspectives of their sources,' she notes. (Source, Cyberschool USA)

The principal benefit of all this is access to vast amounts of useful and up-to-date information in every subject area. Students can also establish meaningful links with other students and take part in a wide range of learning experiences. Their work can be published to an audience of peers and be constructively reviewed.

People are much better, about one million times better in fact, at decoding pictures than lines of words or numbers. Presenting information in a visual form allows us to comprehend it faster and more thoroughly. The new Internet technologies that allow you to 'surf' around millions of pages of pictorial information use that visual processing power to the full.

On-line publishing is developing at a remarkable pace. No longer is it necessary to undertake the expense of type setting and printing to make your material available to your audience. The Internet allows you to communicate on a massive scale. Unfortunately, much of what is published electronically is unusable, but that criticism can be made of printed material too. The SWIFT project, for 5- to 18-year-olds, is an international on-line, live, interactive magazine produced by young people for young people. It covers a wide range of subjects including sport and politics, the environment, food and literature. Groups of pupils take responsibility for editing a section, which involves them in decision-making, editorial skills, and working to deadlines. The end result of their efforts can be viewed on screen by potentially thousands of people worldwide.

Technology in UK schools

How does Britain measure up to the US? The Department for Education and Employment (DfEE) published a report in February 1995 compiled by the Government Statistical Service which surveyed the use of technology in schools. The findings were not encouraging. In 1993-94, for instance, primary schools had to share each computer between 18 pupils; though this was an improvement on the one computer per 25 students a year earlier. As I have already mentioned, a high number of machines per pupil is almost meaningless because it takes no account of the age of the equipment. It is obvious however that our schools are poorly equipped in comparison with a typical office. The quality of software applications and the quality of utilisation by teachers are perhaps even more important but difficult to quantify. The 1995 report found similar shortages in secondary schools. There were, on average, less than 10 computers per school and over half of these were over five years old.

In 1996, an estimated two thousand British schools had a modem, but we don't know the speed of them – and developments have been dramatic in the last 24 months. Today, anything less than 14,400 baud is considered too slow for on-line information services, while 28,800 is becoming the norm. New modems run at 56k, 20 times faster than modems of the early nineties and the cost of high-speed ISDN lines is rapidly approaching the low price of a standard phone connection.

A British project called *Campus World* provides an insight into what can be achieved. BT's *Campus World* is an electronic, on-line educational service currently installed in 4,500 schools, soon expanding to 6,000. It contains an exciting combination of curricular and cross-curricular resources specially created by educationalists for teachers and students, as well as incorporating many features from the Internet. *Campus World* offers a gateway to the Internet using a PC and modem. It allows students to create their own home pages where they design, publish and update their own unique site. The service offers a 'walled garden' where information has been carefully checked for its suitability for schools. Schools can choose to keep within the protected area, or venture out by using a password on to the full Internet.

Access to *Campus World* is by subscription (about £12 per month) while Internet access is extra. The user dials in over the phone line to a local number and communicates with the BT computer that holds the information using a modem and PC computer. Unfortunately there are limitations on the band width of the standard phone lines: in effect, the line is not wide enough to transmit rapidly all the information from the BT computer. There are ways in which the speed of operation could be increased, but there are higher cost implications. An ISDN line, for example, allows access at three to four times the normal speed with installation costs about £120 and an annual rental charge. With the rapid growth of cable television networks the availability of low cost, high speed links to every school are a real possibility in the near future.

Numerous projects are available on *Campus World*. At present the service is the only UK on-line network to offer in-depth curriculum support. Its aim is to help teachers and lecturers deliver the curriculum more effectively in every subject and at every level. Secondary and further education material on the service includes a diverse range – for example, *A-level History* is a computer conference for 16- to 18-year-olds on 20th century international history, which, incorporating guidance from university experts, allows pupils to examine the emergence and role of the UN in its 50th year. In another field, schools and colleges can research cinema history, and negotiate and plan a short film using *Cinema 100*, a collaborative project between France and Britain. Designed for the age range 13 to 19, the material can be integrated into curriculum areas such as media studies, languages, drama, English and history.

Campus World also has material for primary and special needs pupils. *Poetry On-line* is a creative writing activity in which examples of poems in different styles are sent by e-mail. Pupils are encouraged to try their own versions and take part in a 'round robin' in which poems are sent from school to school. *Living in Space* is a cross-curricular project with accompanying resource pack, including teachers' notes and pupils' worksheets. Tasks are sent out by e-mail each day. The *Science Net* allows pupils to send questions on science by e-mail and receive a personal reply from a team of professional scientists. For younger pupils, *Mathsday* offers numerous maths problems each day; *Un, Deux, Trois … On y va!* is a week of activities in French for primary schools including a mystery tour of Paris, Teletel/Minitel (the French precursor to the Internet) experience, a virtual visit to the Louvre and vocabulary lessons. Modern language material for older pupils includes *France à la Carte*, a range of information and projects on France supported by the French Embassy in London, which includes French current affairs, interschool projects and project material for French language study. The Foreign Language News Service brings weekly news from around the world in English, French, German and Spanish and also provides support materials suitable for use by students in higher education.

Rather than computing being viewed as a remote individual exercise these examples illustrate how much interaction there can be between pupils both nationally and internationally. The material will constantly evolve as new students participate and more interesting links are developed through the Internet.

Far from being a threat, the use of on-line technology can open up exciting new areas of learning. Take for example this case history from a tiny rural school, Llanfihangel-y-Creuddyn Primary, in Wales:

'When three of our pupils aged 9-11 measured their temperatures using data-logging equipment while jogging on the spot for two minutes, they found that their temperature dropped before rising, contrary to what they had predicted. Being inquisitive the experiment was repeated for different time intervals up to 20 minutes, with each time interval being run three times. Not being able to explain the results they recorded their findings in a report and e-mailed the problem to *Science Net*. In doing this they recorded their scientific experiment, wrote for a scientific purpose and for an unfamiliar audience, and used electronic communication in what turned out to be a cross-curricular experiment. *Science Net* enabled us in a small, two-teacher, rural school of 40 pupils, without science expertise, to support our pupils in way impossible otherwise and in doing so enriched and broadened their educational experience.'

There is a fear that new software, produced predominantly for the American market, may damage the British cultural heritage, a view expressed for example by Nick Tate, the government's chief curriculum adviser. (*The Times*, 11 June 1996). *Success Master*, an American product, teaches mathematics, English and science requiring pupils to do 15 minutes a day on the computer. The mathematics programme features only dollars and cents and the audio element has an American voice. Teachers are critical of some of the verbal use and also think children's spelling could be muddled. As many television programmes, cartoons and films are American, it seems that there is little that can be done to limit the exposure of Britain's population to it. Despite these criticisms, *Success Master* has been shown to be very effective in improving achievement in mathematics for 7- to 14-year-olds, the age range where there is most concern about declining standards. Francis Howlett, a programme manager at the National Council for Educational Technology, said: 'Children using the programme five days a week for six months were measured against children in the same school not on the system. Those on the system in mathematics showed a 20-month gain in achievement, although there was no significant gain in reading.'

Two further examples concisely illustrate the power of technology. 'In 1987 a budding classicist from the University of Lausanne finished four years of labour. She had spent them scouring ancient Greek tomes searching for the classical source of 2,000 anonymous fragments of medieval text. Then, just when she was getting down to writing her doctoral dissertation, all that effort was eclipsed. In a few dozen hours working with a new database she found every one of her 600 hard-won sources again – and 300 more that had passed her by.' (*The Economist*, 26 August 1994)

The database, *Thesaurus Linguae Grecae*, was one of the first of the tools that are transforming the staid world of what used to be bookish learning. Developed by the University of California, the database covers 3,000 authors and contains 66 million words, all searchable, accessible and printable. One compact disc covers all of this information for approximately $300. Similar databases are available now for a wide range of subjects.

In Britain, the Mercury Helix project allows GPs to call-up patients' records and generate diagrams of different parts of the body, to explain to patients what is wrong with them. The system also allows the user to make an appointment, check the availability of hospital places and treatments, call up professional medical references and send e-mails, for example to check a diagnosis with colleagues.

Such developments as these are not ideas for the future. Rather, they are today's reality for millions of workers in every field. The speed, power and low cost of modern PCs was unimaginable a decade ago. Already new technologies are emerging that may dramatically affect the empires of Bill Gates and other technology leaders of today. For example, new Internet software from Sun Computers radically changes how software is used, so that instead of expensive programmes having to be upgraded by buying the latest edition, Sun's Java software will utilise basic low cost computers that draw on only the software needed at the time, from the global Internet. Television-top computers are coming on to the market too, bringing Internet power to homes for a minimal cost.

The scale of technological change is transforming business, affecting production methods, distribution channels, management and accounting systems and the process of interaction between producer and consumers. Yet the classroom, often locked in a Luddite state of denial, falls further and further behind.

The Electric Library – A Case Study

An exciting educational service, the Electric Library, offers access to comprehensive information including the content of hundreds of magazines and newspapers over the Internet. The service has sophisticated search capabilities and illustrates the power of the Internet to bring the world's knowledge to the home or school. Electric Library is a full-text, multi-subject reference system designed for school students and is very easy to use yet has sophisticated search capabilities. Pupils can examine hundreds of journals and periodicals, newspapers and books within seconds. As one reviewer put it '…(it is) a little ironic that the most innovative on-line service to come along in years is for kids – the least affluent, most overlooked, yet perhaps the most important of on-line users.' The Electric Library includes hundreds of periodicals including *The Economist*, and can be used for an infinitely wide range of research assignments, primarily aimed at the school user. There are more than 150 newspapers and newswire services giving excellent coverage of current events. News sources include the *Los Angeles Times*, *Newsbytes*, *Newsday*, *Philadelphia Tribune*, Reuters, *USA Today*, and *The Washington Times*, and there are plans to include a number of British papers. The content is up to date, often appearing within a day of the printed versions. There are also sections covering numerous foreign and ethnic publications that provide excellent coverage of non-mainstream media and news. The sections covering magazines and journals is even more impressive. There are over 800 including many leading general interest titles such as *American Spectator*, *Christian Century*, *The Economist*, *New Republic* and *Science News*. For more specialised research there are hundreds of professional and academic publications covering a wide range of subjects in business and the humanities. The easy-to-use database covers television and 25,000 radio transcripts and has two encyclopedias, Collier's with 400,000 entries and Funk and Wagnalls that in printed form takes up 29 volumes of general reference material. There is also a world almanac and a cinema database, even the Monarch literary criticism notes are included. Electric Library is not just about text, it includes photographic material with over 25,000 images from a diverse and expanding group of providers including Geosystems and Reuters.

To use Electric Library students need an Internet account and in addition have to pay a fee in the USA of $9.95 each month. For this they can access the database as often as they like and download any amount of information. Queries are typed into a search box and they can consist of single words or complete sentences. The retrieved information appears in a matter of seconds. Ranked in relevancy order, they include the document title, source, date of publication and grade reading level. Clicking on a document or image automatically downloads it. Material can be printed, copied or saved into a word processing document with bibliographic information automatically transferred. This enormous database is being constantly updated each day by satellite and direct links.

Multimedia systems

New technologies already allow video and audio to be transmitted over the Internet and the quality and speed is constantly improving. A typical CD-ROM disc holds the equivalent of 650 paperback books and can be produced for about 20 pence. The entire *Encyclopedia Britannica*, all 44 million words, fits on one CD-ROM disc and costs less than £100. Thousands of new titles are launched each month, and innovative publishers like Dorling Kindersley are producing multimedia CD 'books' that transform the educational process into an exhilarating dynamic environment of interactive sound and pictures.

The most recent advance in CD technology is the development of the CD-I (compact disc-interactive). This technology includes digitized sound, compressed video, animation, and text, creating a multimedia platform for interactive programmes. Sega Genesis, one of the world's leading computer games manufacturers, has already put CD-I on the home video game market ensuring that young people are familiar with this latest technology.

British schools have been slow to take up these new ways of learning. In contrast, multimedia systems have captured the imagination of educators in the US. According to a report by Quality Education Data (QED), 25 per cent of schools' software budgets in the US were allocated to multimedia titles in 1994. The number of computers fitted with CD-ROM drives in American school classrooms has increased dramatically. According to QED, the number has nearly tripled between 1992 and 1995, from 13 per cent to 37 per cent, while more than half of all high schools are now equipped with at least one CD-ROM drive. (*Byte*, March 1995)

Proof of the effectiveness of multimedia systems is not conclusive, but early studies and many anecdotes suggest they have great power as a learning aid. Applications range from educational and entertainment titles to gigantic computational chemistry simulations that run on the powerful Onyx system from Silicon Graphics. One interesting multimedia application called *CamMotion* is being developed by TERC, a research and development organisation in Cambridge, Massachusetts. It uses a visualisation exercise to learn about and analyse physical principles. A video camera lets pupils capture and analyse motion on the computer. One group of students, for instance, used *CamMotion* to understand the difference in acceleration of a basketball when it is dropped and when it is dribbled. Textbook calculus would never have captured the same level of interest.

People obtain 80 per cent of their knowledge visually yet retain only 11 per cent of it, according to Howard Wactlar, vice-provost for research computing at Carnegie Mellon University. A smaller percentage is acquired through hearing, but more of it is remembered. Through a combination of the two, retention rates improve to about 50 per cent. Imagine the impact when thousands of students across the country start to increase their retention levels through the use of new teaching technologies. Pupils' confidence and motivation will increase as they play a more active and successful role in the learning process. Class disruption from bad behaviour could well decline as pupils are stimulated by more dynamic material, and exam success will surely follow.

Language teaching

For many years, foreign language teachers have used the computer to provide supplementary exercises. In recent years, advances in computer technology have motivated some teachers to reassess its use and incorporate it as a valuable part of daily foreign language learning. Innovative software programmes, with authoring capabilities (allowing the computer to check students' written work), compact disc technology, and elaborate computer networks are providing teachers with new methods of incorporating culture, grammar, and real language use in the classroom while students gain access to audio, visual, and textual information about the language and the culture of its speakers. (Higgins, Chris, ERIC Clearinghouse on Languages and Linguistics, Washington, DC, April 1993.)

Traditional language teaching software uses simple drill-and-practice techniques. These programmes focus on vocabulary or particular grammar points. The latest software goes much further than this – modern interactive programmes respond to the needs of the individual student. Simulation programmes present pupils with real-life situations in which they can, for example, learn about the culture of a country and the protocol for various situations. Games, such as the foreign language versions of *Where in the World Is Carmen Sandiego?* by Broderbund Software or *Trivial Pursuit* from Gessler Publishers, provide an entertaining environment for students to learn the target language and the culture of the country through problem-solving and competition. A new dimension, digitised sound, has been incorporated into some of the more advanced language software. The student can record his own speech on the computer's hard drive, enabling him to compare his own pronunciation with that of the original recording on the CD-ROM programme disc.

Using the Internet in school

The Internet gives students access to an enormous range of information on every imaginable subject. The information is constantly expanding and can be searched, sifted and sorted in an infinite number of ways with the minimum cost in time and effort. But this richness of information is both an asset and a liability. Students need to develop new skills in thinking and problem-solving which match the magnitude of the information source. The implications are profound for the teaching profession.

As access to this huge mass of information becomes commonplace, our students will shift from simple memory tests to complex analysis of data to determine patterns and trends and to make inferences. Memorization and regurgitation will be an outdated and redundant practice as pupils develop the critical thinking skills of the researcher and inventor. School work will shift to continuous assessment as students tackle complex questions in a project format. Questions will rarely have right or wrong answers but a series of outcomes, each provoking its own set of new questions and opportunities.

Let me give you an example of the type of question that a group of students might tackle over a term. 'Imagine that you and your partners are consultants hired by the British and Irish governments to recommend new policies to stem the decline of the fish harvests in the Irish Sea during the past decade. Use Internet to identify all useful practices already tested around the globe and then determine the applicability of these practices to the particular conditions and needs of the two countries. Create a multimedia report for the two governments sharing specific action recommendations as well as the evidence sustaining your proposals.'

Schools have traditionally neglected the development of student questioning. According to Hyman (1980), for every 38 teacher questions in a typical classroom there is but one student question. Often student questions come into the 'go and find out about' category that involves little more than gathering basic information rather than any analysis. Pupils need to learn how to move beyond this traditional search for answers to simple questions, towards higher level thinking.

Tomorrow's questions will be far more searching. For example: 'Imagine that your parents have been given job offers in each of the three following cities: Belfast, Edinburgh and Lyon. Knowing of your access to Internet, they have asked you to help them decide which city will be the best for the family to select. Before gathering your information, discuss and identify with them the criteria for selecting a home city. Create a chart showing the strengths and weaknesses of each city on the criteria your family considers important.' Of course a question like this could easily be answered using traditional materials but using Internet the range of answers and the infinite ways of developing the proposals open up exciting opportunities for both pupils and teachers.

Technology and special needs

Technology greatly expands the learning opportunities for those with special needs. For example, the Macintosh and IBM computer-operating system OS2, have a number of special features for those with special needs. When a student has a problem with motor skills repeat keys (the buttons on the computer keyboard that when pressed automatically repeat) can be turned off. There are also large keyboards and mice that make access easier. A headset has been developed, using military technology – when the user turns his head the pointer on the computer screen moves, and by blowing into a tube the operator can click the mouse and use the computer as easily as anyone else.

Computer World's project, SENSOR, provides information over the schools computer system on the seven broad 'difficulties and disabilities', as identified by the UK government, which are faced by learners with special educational needs. The service can also handle personal questions sent by e-mail.

Hull University - An example of good practice

University of Hull, with over 11,000 students, has made a clear commitment to the integration of technology within all its courses, and this, perhaps, is one of the factors that helps the school achieve a high level of graduate employment and one of the lowest student dropout rates in the country. The Vice-Chancellor, Professor David Dilks, wrote in the university publication *Computer Assisted Learning*: 'The University is at the forefront of innovation. In a collegiate-managed university ... there are few areas where technology is not being exploited to enhance the quality and efficiency of teaching, and in some areas, particularly in the area of language learning, the University is doing work of national importance.'

Hull is an excellent example of what can be achieved when there is broad commitment, rather than the more typical passive resistance, to new techniques of learning. Three years ago the University set up a working party to consider ways of promoting the use of educational technology as a means of enhancing both quality and efficiency in teaching and learning. At an early stage in the deliberations of the working party it became apparent that it would be foolish to separate efforts to develop the use of educational technology from more general initiatives to promote quality and innovation in teaching and learning. It was thought that the challenges facing higher education in the 21st century should be met in a rounded way that acknowledged the importance and value of technology, but which also recognised that any new approach should be driven primarily by educational purposes and values.

The Centre for Teaching and Learning Support was established in 1994 to assist in the development and use of learning technology throughout the University. A group of practising academics, from a wide range of disciplinary backgrounds, meets each week to help disseminate information about new learning technologies. The group publishes a newsletter and a variety of documents about innovations in teaching. The Centre also has a presence on the world wide web and provides a wealth of information through this medium.

Hull has introduced modular courses and has a formal requirement for student feedback. Feedback is received through a variety of questionnaires that are wholly electronic using the world wide web. The new system has been used for the main annual assessment of first-year undergraduates in several subjects.

The whole University is encouraged to use the new technologies and there is a diverse range of applications.

New technology has been applied across the disciplinary spectrum. For example, the School of Arts has a postgraduate training programme that offers an introduction to IT for arts students. The course, held in the Arts Microlab, offers postgraduate students basic familiarity with the electronic tools that are considered indispensable to the modern researcher. Even the MA in Medieval Vernacular Languages and Literature has an IT course that teaches students some of the uses of computers in the humanities. Students study a piece of medieval text and present their findings in the form of a hypermedia edition as part of their training in research techniques.

An application by the Department of American Studies illustrates the advantage of technology when applied to academic study. A module focuses on the way in which the United States Supreme Court has helped mould the American socio-economic agenda during the last hundred years. The myriad of American legislative sources is now available on the Internet and up-to-date full text Supreme Court decisions are included making it possible for students to gain access to information in electronic form within a week of a decision, which will not be available in hard copy for another three years. Students can therefore keep up to date with the various contentious and constitutional issues dealt with by the US High Courts which are included in the class module.

The Department of English, in the Introduction to Old English module, includes the use of the hypermedia edition of the Old English (or Anglo-Saxon) poem *The Dream of the Rood*. The poem – a vision of the cross – is a good example of medieval literature in a 'multimedia' context. Students are introduced to the package at a session in the Arts Microlab and the programme is then networked on CALWIN so that students can follow up their work whenever and wherever they wish. In the Creative Writing module, which uses the Computer Centre's conferencing facility, students can e-mail their poetry and prose to each other and their tutor for comment and responses as well as using real time on-line discussion.

In science subjects, new multimedia material is constantly being produced. The School of Chemistry has a CD-ROM Dictionary of Inorganic Compounds that is used as the basis of a 'problem-solving' approach to the teaching of descriptive inorganic chemistry to supplement tutorial lectures. The ability to access the information from any PC on campus greatly enhances its student appeal.

Another area where computers permit learning that is not possible with conventional teaching is in simulation. The School of Life Sciences, Department of Applied Biology, uses SIMLIFE, an ecological simulation that, although developed initially as a game, has proved to be of great educational value. SIMLIFE allows the student to create an environment of his choice and populate it with plants and animals. The student has total control over environmental conditions and can alter the genetic and behavioural patterns of organisms within it. SIMLIFE has no right or wrong answers but allows the student to explore various ecological principles and to examine, for example, the factors that bring about conditions such as global warming.

Hull is an outstanding example of a university with a modern and practical approach to harnessing technology to help all students, whatever their discipline. The benefits will become more apparent to the university's graduates as they enter the work place and find almost every job uses a significant amount of technology.

Evaluation of computer-aided learning

Over the last 15 years, millions of computers have been purchased for schools, yet there have been few studies of the effectiveness of this massive investment. The first computers entered service in schools in the early 1980s and ever since new machines have been purchased as the technology has leapt forward. It is important to ask whether this investment has been beneficial or has it been another educational bandwagon? Has the new technology helped improve the learning process and given pupils a better foundation to use the technology they find at work?

A review of professionally-conducted research, mainly from the US, provides little evidence that growth in skill persists beyond the initial 'gadget stage'. The impact of technology upon such skills is rarely compared with alternative strategies, such as training teachers to be more effective. Too little work has been done in measuring gains in higher order skills, and there have been few studies which explore the growth in student group problem-solving skills. For example, how does the power of students' communication improve when they are taught to compose essays with a word processor or use e-mail on the Internet? No longer do students need to learn formula, they can use powerful statistical software packages in order to gauge relationships between variables. Does this increase comprehension or not?

There is scope for much greater research into the effectiveness of educational technology but, as with all multivariable analysis, assessing cause and effect can give little other than a general indication of the impact.

Schools in the United States in 1995 had an estimated 6 million computers, about one for every nine students. Almost every school in the country had at least one television and videocassette recorder, and almost 50 per cent of all teachers had a television in their classrooms. Only one teacher in eight had a telephone in class, while less than one per cent had access to voice mail. Classroom access to newer technologies, like CD-ROM and networking capabilities, were also limited. While 75 per cent of US public schools have access to some kind of computer network, and 35 per cent of public schools have access to the Internet, only three per cent of instructional rooms (classrooms, labs and media centres) are connected to the Internet.

The federal OTA (Office of Technology Assessment) recently published a disheartening report in the US describing the huge gap between the promise and the reality of technology use by teachers. Despite the level of technology available, a substantial number of teachers report little or no use of computers for instruction. Their use of other technologies also varies considerably. (Most analysis relies on anecdotal or testimonial programme evaluations so the reports tend to highlight successful projects rather than qualitative research findings.)

There are three major uses of technology in education and this compounds the difficulty of assessing the overall impact:

1. To enhance administrative productivity – this includes school accounting software and programmes that monitor student performance. This automation application is found in every business and no doubt schools have enjoyed the benefits that companies have achieved.

2. Automated instruction – using, for example, drill and practice or simulation software. The limited research indicates mixed results with some benefit in improved levels of student motivation.

3. Information processing and productivity – this includes the use of word processors, databases, spreadsheets, presentation programmes and the Internet. The use of these technologies most closely matches work applications, and can provide an excellent foundation for the use of technology when pupils leave school. Using the technology in this way requires significant time investment by teachers. Not only must they

master the often complex programmes themselves, but also spend time developing teaching projects that apply them. Student time is required too and the traditional 20 to 40 minutes in a computer lab each week is insufficient.

Assessment of the value of computer technology is complex. However, the sharing of best practice is one way of encouraging the transmission of innovative ideas and successful implementation of them. As students build up portfolios of project work and spend time in school-to-work transition courses, the value will gradually become apparent.

The Library Media Center, Forest View Elementary School, Mount Prospect, Illinois – a case history

Razzle-Dazzle District: 'morphed' movie images enliven learning in Illinois
by Mary Holden

My grade school days in the 1970s were hardly ancient times. The nuns wore pantsuits, not habits, and we sometimes watched a video in class. But a visit to the Library Media Center at Forest View Elementary School in Mount Prospect, Illinois, made me feel like I did my lessons on clay tablets.

'Don't forget to save,' Dennis Berens warns a fourth-grade class as he crosses to three girls seated at a Macintosh computer. They are preparing a multimedia slide-show presentation on gemstones, complete with voice-overs, graphic transitions that look like exploding bubbles, color backgrounds, and digitized hand-drawn pictures and photographs. 'It's not the old push-the-pencil-across-the-paper thing,' says Berens, who directs the media center, pointing out the obvious. The computers 'make kids really want to come down and do this ... It's exciting for them ... They just eat it up.'

Community Consolidated School District 59 (K-8; enrollment 6,400) began a major effort in computer technology about five years ago, Berens explains. Supported by the growing tax base of Chicago's industrial suburbs, as well as by state and corporate grants, District 59 has rapidly become one of the leading users of computer technology in the state – and was honored for that achievement last year by the National Education Association.

District schools have as many as four computers per classroom and banks of computers in every library. Rooms in renovated buildings have large overhead monitors that teachers use for 'electronic chalkboards'. Teachers in non-renovated buildings can wheel oversized monitors into their rooms. A repertoire of software, including *Kid Pix* (Broderbund Software), *Hyper Studio* (Roger Wagner Publishing), *MediaText* (Wings for Learning), and *Power Point* (Microsoft), and tools such as laser disc movies aid instruction in every subject and every grade.

Since July, the district has had its own Internet node, a server that connects it to information resources around the world. And links between the server and all 13 schools, through a wide-area network, are expected to be completed this spring.

Behind District 59's plunge into cyberspace is Associate Superintendent for Instruction Robert Bortnick, an avuncular ex-college teacher with a contagious enthusiasm for computers. Bortnick's love for computers began 30 years ago as a graduate student at the University of Chicago. 'I was taught by a 12-year-old,' he says.

But the district's focus, Bortnick emphasizes, is on using technology as a learning tool, not on teaching how to use technology *per se*. '(We're) talking about giving kids a tool which they can use to leverage and extend their learning capabilities,' he says. 'That's what I think is going to distinguish kids who are competitive in a global information society.'

The need to equip kids for a high-tech future might be why Bortnick thinks the district should spend a lot more on technology than the $400,000 it budgeted last year. That amount, at less than one per cent of the total district budget (which averages $7,000 per pupil) is 'too little', he says. And further growth will require tough policy choices, because changes in state tax laws will make it hard to raise school spending in the years ahead.

Yet Bortnick does have a few funding cards up his sleeve – corporate and state grants that added $250,000 to technology coffers last year and helped finance, among other things, a new technology training center. Grantors are impressed by the district's demonstrated commitment to technology, Bortnick says.

That commitment is multifaceted, because all the new equipment wouldn't mean much without staff training, long-term planning, creative teachers able to work the technology into the curriculum, and a commitment to using the computers as a means, not an end, Bortnick says. 'Our success in part is due to the fact that we're really not interested in the boxes and the wires; it's what you can do to help deliver instruction.' Certain teachers have 'really provided leadership', he adds, some of them by creating innovative computer-learning programmes in the days when the district had only a few computers.

And the planning component also has deep roots. Bortnick says planning for the district's current level of usage took several years and included extensive input from a citizens' committee. John Prusko, who teaches science at Elk Grove Junior High School and provides technical support for the district, agrees that planning is a key to the success of a large-scale computer initiative. 'You need a five-year plan, you need community support,' Prusko says.

Jacquelyn Karlin, a kindergarten teacher at the John Jay School in Mount

Prospect, underlines the importance of staff training: 'If you don't train your teachers to do it, they're not going to do it. I had time to create these (programmes for class), and I had the training. If we didn't have that, we could have the computers and not do anything.'

Bortnick admits that staff development started late and has been spotty. 'A lot of training, unfortunately, is (a) one-shot deal,' he says, 'and while that creates awareness I don't know that it always creates competence.' To tackle the training problem, the district has introduced a variety of programs. One is an annual summer programme that trains children in creating multimedia projects and provides a staff development opportunity for teachers. 'They get training, and (they) work with students, and afterward they feel really comfortable,' Bortnick says. Staff members also attend programmes after school at the district's new training center; and individual schools set aside time each week for training during school hours. In addition, teachers can look for help on the district's home page.

Media centre director Berens explains the other end of the spectrum – how first-graders at Forest View Elementary study the concept of 'community'. Students take home a school camcorder, and their parents use it to videotape objects in the community, such as a tall building. The teacher records each child's voice describing the object, and the class collection of video clips is compiled into a presentation that is shown to the students.

Teachers also combine commercial products with presentations developed in-house. Karlin, for example, teaches her kindergarteners about language and music using a commercial *Pocahontas* laser disc and the lyrics to the movie's songs stored on a floppy disk. She projects the lyrics on an overhead monitor and highlights words with a computer mouse, or she creates an electronic marker to follow along with the voice on the laser disc. She can return easily to a certain word or phrase, a feat that would be cumbersome with a tape recorder.

Karlin, who has taught kindergarten for 25 years and has written her own software programmes for the past five years, believes the computer lets her be more creative. And the multimedia capabilities, she says, help children who learn in different ways: 'It's audio, it's video, it's tactile, they can dance to it. Everyone learns in a different way, and this kind of brings it altogether.'

Students at many grade levels use popular software such as *Kid Pix* for school projects, like the slide show on gems. Teachers put together their own multimedia presentations. When Prusko taught about atomic energy, for example, he could show a laser disc film of an A-bomb being loaded on to an airplane. 'I have to keep the kids' attention,' says Prusko, who has taught for 29 years. 'For all practical purposes, we're competing with all the electronic equipment they have at home.'

Laser discs and high-capacity computers allow students even to manipulate movie images. Bortnick demonstrates a new scene he created for *Star Wars* with the help of some students: it ends with Luke Skywalker's face morphing into his own. 'I always wanted to be Luke Skywalker,' he jokes.

Students and teachers use the Internet to find information and to download images for projects. But teachers arguably have less time for 'surfing', so last summer, a group of teachers compiled a 'hot list' of good-quality world wide web sites in 60 or 70 curriculum areas – such as native American studies. The list helps teachers jump swiftly to detailed information, for example, on native American literature, culture, and history. Other sites, such as the home page of Chicago's Field Museum, have terrific student activities there for the taking, Bortnick says.

Students and teachers also communicate with other schools. For example, through a programme sponsored by the National Geographic Society, third-graders work via the Internet with students around the United States on solving the nation's waste disposal problem.

District 59 has begun using the Internet for video conferences. 'We talk to people all over the world – young, old, kids in school, people in college,' says Stephanie Shintani, age 15. Shintani took part in that activity before she graduated from District 59; now a high school sophomore, she still hangs around the administration building, helping Bortnick prepare multimedia presentations. She says she enjoys researching and preparing school projects on a computer as opposed to using a book and a binder. 'It's a lot different; you learn, I think, a lot more,' she says. 'There are so many more resources … You get to use different media, you can use sound and pictures – it gets you into the project more.'

District 59 educators, like school leaders elsewhere, are having to come up with solutions to the new problems the Internet raises. For example, the district keeps children away from material that isn't educational and age-appropriate by using 'firewalls' and by granting Internet access as a privilege, Bortnick says. The district also chooses not to carry news groups – public on-line discussion groups that in some cases feature pornography – on its server.

Nothing is foolproof, however, and a few students have come across a site inadvertently, Bortnick says. He did so himself, when he tried to find a picture of fluffy yellow chicks for a kindergarten teacher. On an Internet search programme he typed 'chicks' and came up with the other kind. 'I'm glad I didn't do it in front of the kindergarten class,' he laughs, adding that the district is looking at software that will block out additional unwanted material.

A key advantage of the wide-area network is that teachers have easier access to reference materials. Formerly, to draw from the district's collection of laser discs and videos, which are stored at the central office, teachers looked up items in a big yellow book, completed an order slip, and sent it in. Now the collection is searched and the request made by computer, Bortnick says, and the use of the reference materials has increased 'dramatically'.

Teachers' comfort level with the technology is mixed, says Berens. 'For the most part, everyone is very accepting of it.' He underlines the benefit of ongoing training programmes and support staff who help with problems. Still, he says, some teachers feel overwhelmed by the amount of new technology and information. Karlin, on the other hand, doesn't think teachers are uncomfortable, just at different levels of proficiency. 'Some people are creating; some people are using the programmes that exist,' Karlin says. 'Everybody knows how to use it. Everybody uses it in a way (he or she is) comfortable with.'

Of course, worrying about people's comfort level is a condition that other districts with fewer resources would love to have. Bortnick advises that technology costs less than some schools think. A modem costs under $200; high-quality CD-ROMS can be had for $19 to $49; and prices of most kinds of hardware continue to fall.

Considering how important computers have become to the world, Bortnick says schools should be rethinking how they spend their money. 'Do we really need to invest as much as we have in the past in a textbook that's going to be dated pretty immediately?' he asks. 'Do I have to spend the kind of money that libraries have spent ... for subscription materials and reference materials?' Certainly, District 59 is actively addressing those questions – and its priorities will never be quite the same.

Another case history
Rural Revolution – A small school takes big strides with technology
by Danny Shaw, Principal of Aiken Elementary School in South Carolina

Nestled near the gateway to South Carolina's sandy Atlantic flatlands, Aiken Elementary isn't in the kind of community where you'd expect to find a technology revolution. Much of the community is rural, and poverty is a stark reality for many of our children. More than a third of our students receive free or reduced-price lunches.

Yet educators come from all over the country to see what we're doing here. We are showing that technology can have a demonstrable effect on achievement in a school where 37 percent of the students are minorities. *Redbook* magazine recently named our school one of the 142 best elementary schools in the country, and the best one in South Carolina; and Aiken Elementary has been recognised as a national school of excellence by the US Department of Education.

But if I credited our success entirely to technology, I would be giving technology far more credit than it deserves. We have a 97 per cent attendance rate among our teaching staff, and our teachers are the ones who make the connections between learning and technology work on a daily basis.

What I can safely say, though, is I believe the technology we've incorporated into school life has been one of the major reasons for our success. I believe it's a big reason our average scores on reading, math, science, and language tests are well above district and state averages.

For instance, last year 66 per cent of our fourth-graders scored above the 50th percentile on a standardised reading test, compared with 44 per cent district wide and 37 per cent statewide. We also scored way ahead of district and state averages on standardised math and language tests. To top it off, Aiken has maintained a student-attendance rate of 96 per cent or higher for the past three years.

And we've accomplished all this without overburdening our taxpayers. Our cost per student is $3,822, which is about $2,000 below the national average. In other words, without spending tons of money, we've found a way to encourage our kids to want to come to school; and most important, once they get here, they learn.

Achieving our goals

We have what I believe is perhaps the most advanced elementary school technology system in South Carolina. Not surprisingly, we are often mistaken for being a magnet school for technology or for gifted students, when, in reality, the school reflects the population of a small southern town.

But when you walk into our school, you realise we are anything but average. We have 400 IBM computers for 873 students, software packages tailored to each academic discipline, CD-ROM, state-of-the-art technologies for music and the arts, connections to the Internet, Compuserve, a variety of electronic bulletin boards and e-mail systems, and the only distance-learning satellite dish found in an elementary school anywhere in the state.

All this did not come about overnight. We spend a good amount of time hustling for grants to find the money to maintain what we're doing, and each year, we do a little more. Of the 1,060 public schools in South Carolina, Aiken is one of only six to win incentive awards from the state education department every year for the past 10 years. We got nearly $400,000 from those grants alone.

What we also have from the state department of education – which I see as vital to our success – is status as a deregulated school. In other words, we are free of most of the mandates that place constraints on how a school uses its time. And the way we use our time is a key to the link between technology and student achievement.

For instance, the state requires 175 minutes a week of social studies for students. If we had to adhere to those types of constraints, we would not be able to require that every student spend at least 20 minutes a day working on school projects in our computer lab. Yet we do exactly that.

Why? Because we want to make sure that technology is a daily part of our students' education. The school has computer terminals and workstations in every classroom, but we know time won't permit all students to use those every day. That's why we build in the 20 minutes of lab time every day for every student.

Two classes are scheduled simultaneously in the 64-computer lab. During that time, classroom teachers remain in the lab with students, along with two technology specialists assigned to the lab. This means we often have a ratio of one adult for every 10 or 12 students, which allows our staff to offer more individual attention. We have from four to six computers in each of our classrooms, which have about 22 students per class.

The pervasive approach

But that is just one way in which we try to infuse technology into school life. Also, our entire building is networked. This allows students to continue working on the same projects before, during, and after their scheduled lab times. They can access the same project from the lab or their classroom.

Again, time, and how it is used, becomes an important issue. If students and teachers were boxed into scheduled holes that determine how long they could devote to a particular subject, students would not have as many opportunities to use interactive video or CD-ROM to explore a science problem, or to use the technology-assisted music software to learn to read music and play a keyboard.

Our music classroom has 30 computer workstations. Research tells us that students who study music develop analytical skills that make them better thinkers. We think technology has sparked a rebirth of interest in music education for all students. And the new technologies seem to get kids more interested in music, whether they are gifted musicians or not.

The school's media center is fully equipped with an automated check-out system that allows students to log on from classroom computers, and check out materials. A video lab comparable to what you might see in a commercial television studio is also part of the media center. All classrooms have color televisions, and programmes can be taped in the video lab and played throughout the building on the school's distribution system and in-house television channels. We have even created a video newsletter we send to parents.

Foreign language programmes have also been improved by the infusion of technology. All our fifth-grade students learn German, and we use our satellite dish to broadcast German television programmes into our classrooms from stations in Germany.

All guidance and administrative records are kept in the school's computer network, and special-needs students' individualised education plans are generated by computer, which saves the special-education staff untold hours.

So, technology is not just an add-on at Aiken. It is an integral part of the daily lives of students and teachers – so much so that I think we have created a 'school of tomorrow'. And I truly believe that a school of tomorrow has students who want to learn in school today.

Chapter Eight
The Future for Higher Education

'Cauliflower is nothing but cabbage with a college education.'
Mark Twain (1835–1910), *Puddinhead Wilson*

In 1995 the British committee of Vice-Chancellors and Principals reported that 25,000 students dropped out of higher education for financial reasons. Perhaps this is true but many may have left for other reasons – finding the work too hard or too dull or just leaving to get a job.

The modular approach, the patterns of credit accumulation used in the United States and by the Open University, is a much more sensible way for students to work through their course material. Students would be better able to drop out and come back in as their life circumstances changed. Such a system would be much more in tune with the life-long learning and personal development needs of today's individual. Of course it might challenge the arbitrary 'ivory tower' rigour of those running our academic institutions, but isn't it time to meet the needs of society and the 'customer'? As Kate Orebi Gann of Marks & Spencer said to the AGR Conference in 1995, 'There is also a healthy view that even if people drop out, for whatever reason, it is better to have experienced some time in higher education than none at all. We must guard against branding them as failures.'

Ernest Boyer, the educationalist and former president of the Carnegie Foundation, saw the main impediment to achieving real changes in the education system lay between the high schools and their relationship (or lack of it) with higher education institutions. His work on American undergraduates was considered the most systematic study ever attempted. The American college, he concluded, was 'a troubled institution ... driven by careerism and more successful in credentialising than in providing a quality education.' Similarly, Elliot Eisner of Stanford University commented, 'Universities focus on the "methodologically neat" to publish in journals that are never read.'

Is it possible to build a virtual university where students, teachers and learning material come together only in cyberspace? It appears so. The School of Continuing Education at New York University has embarked on such a project using powerful software such as Lotus Notes and high speed ISDN digital phone lines. The NYU Virtual College, begun in 1992, offers a small number of courses taught entirely in virtual classrooms. Each student owns a Windows PC and a modem. Using the powerful Lotus Notes software, that allows computer users to share information, students receive electronic lectures that are delivered as multimedia presentations, obtain required course readings, contribute to discussion topics, and send e-mail to one another and the instructor. Participation in the programme costs about $2,000.

Currently, the Virtual College is used mainly for mid-career training. Scheduled classes are especially difficult for those who are working and taking classes in the evening and on part-time courses. The Virtual College lets people attend anywhere and at any time. The NYU programme has an additional attribute that bears on its success. The subject matter of the courses consists of applied information systems and virtual work groups, so that students are gaining not only theoretical knowledge of the topic but also practical hands-on experience of teleworking, an increasingly popular concept in America.

One surprising result of the programme is the effect on student participation. The amount of interaction among students, and between students and instructors, is of an order of magnitude higher than that of the normal classroom. This is measured by observing how many questions are asked and the liveliness of the discussion threads. Of course distance learning is not a new concept – but what makes the NYU model so interesting is the participative or interactive nature of the learning process. Unlike a night-school class, students can attend at a time that suits their lives and can be in different cities or even different countries.

Pepperdine University, one of America's top 50 liberal arts schools, has a new doctoral programme in educational technology. Students have been recruited nationwide to come in for eight days of study with the faculty and then go back to their homes and continue the course on-line on the computer. As students prepare papers they can discuss books and readings on-line with faculty members and with each other. The use of on-line technology allows Pepperdine to utilise the resources of the faculty and involve students from all over the country, but still offer a highly personalised approach. The course has been a great success, with reports of a strong team spirit and an exciting atmosphere for the individuals involved. Professors from across the country join the course for on-line discussion with graduate students. Other tracks are in institutional management and in organisation development. A virtual library allows full text access to 6,000 journals and periodicals that can be called up on computer screens.

This book is about reform of the primary and secondary school system. These brief examples of innovative practices in higher education illustrate the new opportunities that school leavers may have. Schools need to adapt their own teaching methods to prepare school leavers not only for employment but to ensure that they have the foundation skills to come back to higher education when the time is right for them.

Technology is transforming the way we work and these changes will in time sweep though education. Teachers, politicians, parents and government agencies can't ignore the shift and will have to adapt to ensure they serve the needs of future generations.

Chapter Nine
Conclusion

There are no simple answers as to how to improve our education system, yet most would agree that we can do much better. When questioned about how he would improve his school's performance from 45 per cent five A-C passes, the headmaster of Garibaldi School summed up the challenges as 'more good staff, high quality teacher appraisal on an annual basis, strong administrative systems and a change in culture of parents and children to believe in the importance of education'.

Clearly there will always be people who are unemployed despite their desire for work. By restructuring school curricula from the perspective of the demands of the world of work, teachers can help reduce the gap between the inadequate skills levels of many young people and those needed to gain employment in an increasingly complex society.

The term 'integration' sums it up best. In reality, all of the management and culture issues outlined in this book are important. In striving to turn out the premium product – well-rounded young people who can use their talents fully – we must be wary of making a distinction between an academic and a vocational education. Having skills that are of use in the work place does not mean abandoning academia. The two categories of vocational and academic knowledge must be combined so that young people are encouraged to develop the widest set of skills possible. By combining academic knowledge and vocational ability true value can be gained from our education system. The child gifted in mathematics must be able to understand the essentials of working in a metal shop, while the gifted craftsman should leave school having studied literature. If this goal is not attained, we are in danger of producing one-dimensional people, the less fortunate of whom will achieve only a level of skills and attitudes that will guarantee exclusion for them from the benefits of our developed society.

Every young person who leaves school has achieved something. It is impossible to have learned nothing, even if you have no piece of paper to show for 12 or more years of compulsory education. Others have suggested, and I support the view, that school leavers should have a portfolio of work that can be presented to prospective employers, demonstrating the whole range of achievements accomplished during their school years. Nobody should leave school saying 'there is nothing that I can do, I am a failure'.

The challenge facing politicians and educationalists is how to adapt to the needs of a world that is changing faster than man has ever before experienced. Progress demands new solutions to new problems and involves experimentation, risk-taking and innovation in a climate of uncertainty. Those responsible need courage and confidence to deliver.

Whether Perelman is right when he says that 'the nations that stop trying to reform their education and training institutions and choose instead to totally replace them with a brand-new, high-tech learning system will be the world's economic powerhouses through the 21st century', or whether there is room to integrate the best of our current thinking with the possibilities opened by new technologies, remains to be seen.

Improving Links with Business
Teacher Check List

1. Contact local employers to find those interested in a relationship with your school.
2. Arrange class visits to local employers.
3. Organise a project for students to visit a local company and report on the job skills the company is likely to need when the students enter the labour market.
4. Invite local employers to visit the school to explain the types of job which may be available and the characteristics they seek in employees.
5. Provide employers with a noticeboard in the school to advertise job opportunities.
6. Invite parents who are employed to come and describe their work and qualifications to students.
7. Ask companies for copies of promotional material that shows the type of work undertaken.
8. Review the existing curriculum to see how it could be modified to better equip students for work.
9. Find out what software is used by local companies and offer students classes in the use of those programmes.
10. Keep in contact with business support organisations including the local Business Link, Chamber of Commerce, TEC and Department for Industry.

Bibliography and Other Sources

Davis, R. C. (1992, March). *Multimedia support for studies in foreign language and culture.* IBM Higher Education: Supplement to THE Journal, March, 1992

Education and Employment Opportunities for Young People, Labour Party 1996

Education and Training for 14-19-Year-Olds. Vol.1, Session 1995-96. House of Commons Education Committee. HMSO, 1996.

Eggen, Paul A. *Educational Psychology* Macmillan Publishing, New York 1992.

Eisner, E.W. *The Educational Imagination* 2nd ed. MacMillan, New York 1985.

The Formation of Young People's Attitudes Towards Business and Industry University of Oxford Department of Educational Studies for Industry in Education and the Design Council, undated

Gardner, Howard *Multiple Intelligences: The Theory in Practice* Basic Books, 1993

Garrett, N. *Technology in the service of language learning: Trends and issues* Modern Language Journal, pp 75, 74-101, 1991.

Glines, Don, *Creating Educational Futures* Michigan, McNaughton and Gunn, 1995.

Grand Met Trust *What Employers Want from the School or College Leaver* UK 1995.

Handy, Charles *Beyond Certainty* Hutchinson, London, 1995.

Higgins, Chris *Computer-Assisted Language Learning: Current Programs and Projects* ERIC Digest. ERIC Clearinghouse on Languages and Linguistics, Washington, DC, April 1993

Jamieson, Ian and Lightfoot, Martin *Schools and Industry: Derivations from the Schools Council Industry Project* Methuen Educational, London, 1982.

King, Al *Synthesis of Information Relating to School and Business Partnerships* Office of Educational Research, Washington, DC, 1986.

Krause, J. *Telecommunications in foreign language education: A resource list.* ERIC Digest. Washington, DC: ERIC Clearinghouse on Languages and Linguistics. 1989.

Lewis, Martyn. *Go for It!* Lennard Publishing, England, 1991 (Revised annually)

Little, Judith Warren *The Compressed Curriculum: Compromise of Purpose and Content in Secondary Schools* National Center for Research in Vocational Education, Berkeley, CA. 1992.

National Council for Educational Technology *Information Technology Stimulate to Educate*, NCET Coventry 1994.

Northcutt, Norvell *Adult Functional Competency: A Summary* The University of Texas, Division of Extension, Austin, 1975.

Perelman, Lewis J. *School's Out* Avon Books, New York, 1992.

Peyton, J.K., and Batson, T. *Computer networking: Making connections between speech and writing.* ERIC/CLL News Bulletin, 10(1), pp 1-6, 1986.

Prince's Youth Business Trust, *Unemployment Trends 91-93* Private Publication. UK.

SCANS Report. *What work requires of schools America 2000* The Secretary's Commission on Achieving Necessary Skills, US Department of Labor. June 1991.

Tyler, Ralph W. *Basic Principles of Curriculum and Instruction* University of Chicago Press, 1949.

Understanding Industry/University of Derby. *Research into knowledge of, and attitudes towards, industry amongst 16-19-year-old students.* Feb. 1995.

Willetts, K. *Integrating technology into the foreign language curriculum: A teacher training manual.* Washington: Center for Applied Linguistics.

Young Enterprise. Internal Performance Report. Unpublished. UK 1993.

Other Sources of Information

1. Publications

Ascher, Carol and Flaxman, Erwin, *A Time for Questions: The Future of Integration and Tech Prep* New York: Institute on Education and the Economy, 1993.

Braunger, Jane and Hart-Landsberg Sylvia, *Crossing Boundaries: Explorations in Integrative Curriculum* Portland, Oregon: Northwest Regional Education Laboratory, 1994.

Case Study Evaluations Washington, DC: US General Accounting Office/Program Evaluation and Methodology Division, 1987.

Center for Workforce Preparation. *On Target: Effective Parent Involvement Programs* Washington, DC, Author, 1994.

Computer-Mediated Collaborative Learning: An Empirical Evaluation MIS Quarterly, June 1994, pp. 159-174, Maryam Alavi, College of Business and Management, University of Maryland.

Conners, Lori J. and Epstein, Joyce L. *Taking Stock: Views of Teachers, Parents, and Students on School, Family, and Community Partnerships in High Schools* Baltimore: Center on Families, Communities, Schools & Children's Learning, 1994.

Cornell Youth and Work Program. *A Parent's Guide to Youth Apprenticeship* Ithaca, NY: Cornell University, 1994.

Fetterman, D. M., Kaftarian, S.J., and Wandersman A. *Empowerment Evaluation: Knowledge and Tools for Self-Assessment and Accountability* Newbury Park, CA: Sage Publications, 1995.

Fink, A. *Evaluation for Education and Psychology* Newbury Park, CA: Sage Publications, 1995.

Gibbons, C.T. *How to Assess Program Implementation* Center for the Study of Evaluation, UCLA. Newbury Park, CA: Sage Publications, 1987.

Grubb, W. Norton, ed. *Education Through Occupations in American High Schools* Volumes I & II. Williston, VT: Teachers College Press, 1995.

Hanushek, Eric, Burtless, Gary (Ed) *Does Money Matter? The Effect of School Resources on Student Achievement and Adult Success* Brookings Institute Press, Washington DC, 1996.

Integrated Learning Atlanta, GA: Southern Regional Education Board, 1995.

Jobs for the Future, Inc. *Voices from School and Home: Pennsylvania Students and Parents Talk About Preparing for the World of Work and a Youth Apprenticeship Program.* Somerville, MA: Author, 1990.

King, J. A., Morris, L.L. and Fitz-Kreuger, R. *Focus Groups: A Practical Guide for Applied Research* Newbury Park, CA: Sage Publications, 1988.

Littel, J. H. *Building Strong Foundations* Chicago: The Family Resource Coalition, 1986.

Orr, M. T. *Evaluating School-to-Work Transition* Washington, DC: Academy for Educational Development, 1995.

Rich, Dorothy *Megaskills* New York: Houghton Mifflin Company, 1992.

Roegge, Chris A., Galloway, James R, and Wegle, Julie A *Setting The Stage: A Practitioner's Guide to Integrating Vocational and Academic Education* Springfield, IL: Illinois State Board of Education, 1991.

Rossi, P. H., and Freeman, H.E. *Evaluation: A Systematic Approach* Newbury Park, CA: Sage Publications, 1993.

Schmidt, B. June, Curtis, R. Finch, and Faulkner, Susan L *Teachers' Role in the Integration of Vocational and Academic Education* Berkeley, CA: The National Center for Research in Vocational Education, 1992.

School-to-Work Toolkit: Building a Local Program Cambridge, MA: Jobs for the Future, 1994.

Shipman, S. *General Criteria for Evaluating Social Programs* Evaluation Practice 10:1 (February 1989).

Worthen, B. R., and Sanders, J.R. *Educational Evaluation: Alternative Approaches and Practical Guidelines* White Plains, NY: Longman Publishers, 1987.

2. Organisations

Alternative Schools Network (ASN) supports community-based and community-run programmes that develop and expand educational, training, and support services for youth – particularly for youth in inner-city neighbourhoods. Much of ASN's work has involved assisting in the development of programmes for out-of-school youth or those at risk of dropping out. 1807 West Sunnyside, Suite 1D, Chicago, IL 60640, (312) 728-4030.

Association for Supervision & Curriculum Development (ASCD) is an international community of educators dedicated to the improvement of instructional supervision, instruction, and curriculum design. ASCD disseminates information on education research and classroom practices and forges links among educators through publications and training programmes, seminars and conferences. ASCD is particularly interested in the general topic of curriculum integration and has sponsored both publications and conferences on this subject. 1250 North Pitt Street, Alexandria, VA 22314-1453. (703) 549-9110.

Center for Human Resources (CHR) at Brandeis University seeks to improve the quality of employment preparation and education services by combining knowledge gained from scholarly research and practical experience in ways that help policy makers successfully address the issues of long-term self-sufficiency for youth and young adults. CHR has assisted thousands of policy makers and practitioners to create community-wide strategies linking education reform, workforce preparation, and economic development. 60 Turner Street, Waltham, MA 02154. (617) 736-3770. hn4032@handsnet.org.

Center for Law and Education's VOCED Project works with schools and communities to develop school-to-work systems and improve occupational education programmes. The VOCED Project publishes policy papers as well as practical guidelines and conducts workshops and conferences on how to improve programs. 1875 Connecticut Avenue, NW, Suite 510, Washington, DC 20009. (202) 986-3000.

Center of Occupational Research and Development (CORD) is a service organisation that helps educators in schools and industry address the technical education, training, and retraining needs of workers. A primary organisational focus is the development of applied academic curricula. Among the curricula available from CORD are Applied Mathematics, Applications in Biology/Chemistry, Principles of Technology, and Tech Prep Resources. 601 Lake Air Drive, P.O. Box 21689, Waco, TX 76702-1689. (817) 772-8756.

Center on Education and Work at the University of Wisconsin is a research, development, and technical assistance unit of the university's school of education whose mission is to improve the linkage between education and work to ensure that all citizens engage in meaningful and productive careers. The Center develops new knowledge through research, designs and evaluates innovations, and translates research and development findings into practical solutions and effective policies through capacity-building technical assistance and dissemination. 964 Educational Sciences, 1025 West Johnson, Madison, WI 53706. (608) 263-3696. aphelps@mail.soemadison.wisc.edu.

Education Development Center, Inc. (EDC) is an international non-profit-making research and development organisation whose projects span the globe, joining research with practice to meet challenges in education, health, technology, human rights, and the environment. EDC's National School-to-Career Consortium is a collaborative of 21 education, industry, labour, research, state government, post-secondary education, and community-based organisations established to provide technical assistance to school-to-work programmes and systems. 55 Chapel Street, Newton, MA 02158-1060. (617) 969-7100. joycem@edc.org.

The mission of the Far West Laboratory for Educational Research and Development (FWL) is to challenge and enable educational organisations and their communities to create and sustain improved learning and development opportunities for their children, youth, and adults. FWL conducts research and evaluations, develops products and programmes, provides assistance to education agencies at all levels, communicates the results of research and exemplary practice, and explores linkages among other agencies and institutions. 730 Harrison Street, San Francisco, CA 94107-1226. (415) 565-3000. sananda@fwl.org.

Institute on Education and the Economy (IEE) at Columbia University is a multi-disciplinary research and technical assistance centre. IEE conducts research on the implications of changes in the economy and labour markets for all levels of education and training systems in the United States. The Institute also provides technical assistance and evaluation services to schools, school districts, and states involved in work-related education reform. Teachers College, Box 174, 525 West 120th Street, New York, NY 10027. (212) 678-3091. iee@columbia.edu.

KRA Corporation is a small business professional and technical services organisation. Its research and development division focuses on the application of the social and behavioural sciences to support policy making, planning, service delivery, and management, particularly in the area of youth programmes. KRA's client divisions include research and evaluation, organisational consulting, information technology, and communications and management. 1010 Wayne Avenue, Suite 850, Silver Spring, MD 20910. (301) 495-1591. infosys@KRA.com.

National Center for Research in Vocational Education (NCVRE) was established under the Carl D. Perkins Vocational Education Act to sponsor applied research and development in the field of occupational education. NCRVE has funded a variety of projects and published several reports on integrated curricula. University of California at Berkeley, 1995 University Avenue, Suite 375, Berkeley, CA 94704. (510) 642-4004.

National Center on the Educational Quality of the Workforce is a national research and development centre concerned with workforce and education issues, which examines the interaction of employers, schools, students/workers, and public policy to determine how better connections among these stakeholders would improve the educational quality of the workforce and bolster the nation's competitiveness in a global economy. University of Pennsylvania, 4200 Pine Street, 5A, Philadelphia, PA 19104-4090. (215) 898-4585. eqw-requests@irhe.upenn.edu.

National Consortium for Product Quality (NCPQ) is a project funded by the National Center for Research in Vocational Education and directed by the Center on Education and Work, University of Wisconsin-Madison. The NCPQ was established to accomplish a two-fold mission: one, to develop, research, and implement school-to-work product standards; and two, to develop a national review process by which school-to-work materials can be collected, evaluated, and disseminated. Center on Education and Work, 964 Education Sciences Building, 1025 West Johnson Street, Madison, WI 53706. (608) 263-3152. bdoughertyper centcew@soemadison.wisc.edu.

National Dropout Prevention Center (NDPC) works with teachers, counsellors, administrators, businesses, and community leaders concerned with dropout issues. NDPC provides technical assistance to programmes operating dropout prevention programmes; conducts research on a variety of dropout and dropout-related issues; and collects, analyses, and disseminates information on dropout prevention strategies. NDPC also operates a database listing programmes and other resources applicable to at-risk youth. Many of their services and resources are directed at out-of-school as well as in-school at-risk youth. 205 Martin Street, Clemson, SC 29634-5111, (803) 656-2599.

National Network for Curriculum Coordination In Vocational and Technical Education (NCCVTE) is a nationwide network of six curriculum coordination centres sponsored by the US Department of Education, Office of Vocational and Adult Education. The network promotes sharing of curricula, professional development of state and local educators, research in curriculum design methodology, and coordination of development among states.

Network, Inc. is a non-profit-making organisation formed to link innovative schools in Massachusetts with each other. The Center for Learning, Technology, and Work, a division of The Network, helps schools and districts that are developing school-to-work efforts. In order to support teachers and administrators who are designing new programmes, the Centre provides assistance on implementing school-to-work strategies, restructuring high school curricula to support workplace learning, introducing technology education programmes, and integrating academic and occupational education. 300 Brickstone Square, Suite 900, Andover, MA 01810. (508) 470-1080.

Rindge School of Technical Arts, Cambridge Rindge and Latin High School, 459 Broadway, Cambridge, MA 02138. (617) 349-6752.

Southern Regional Education Board's High Schools That Work programme, operated by SREB's State Vocational Education Consortium, aims to improve the education of students enrolled in high school occupational programmes at more than three dozen pilot sites. The consortium develops, applies, evaluates, and promotes strategies to strengthen students' competencies in communications, mathematics, science, critical thinking, and problem-solving. 592 Tenth Street, NW, Atlanta, GA 30318-5790. (404) 875-9211.

YouthBuild USA is a comprehensive youth and community development programme that provides unemployed high school dropouts with the opportunity to serve their communities as they develop job skills and prepare for their future. Participants build housing for the homeless and other low-income people while attending a YouthBuild-operated school to earn a high-school equivalency degree and perhaps prepare to continue into post secondary education. Programming includes intensive group counselling and peer support networks. YouthBuild USA also provides technical assistance to local organisations either operating or planning to implement a YouthBuild programme. 58 Day Street, Third Floor, West Somerville, MA 02144, (617) 623-9900

Index